PARABLES: REWIRED

MIKE ELMS

CONTENTS:

FOREWORD:
BY MARK GREENE

Mike Elms used to work in advertising.

Don't hold it against him.

Actually, he worked in the same agency as I did. He stayed longer, soared higher, and was at the helm at a time when it had one of the highest reputations for honesty and integrity in the industry. Everything is relative, you might say.

Still, you can see Mike's understanding of succinct, attitude-changing, behaviour-changing communication and his integrity in this eye-opening, heart-lifting, Jesus-loving book. After all, most of the parables can be told in about the same time as your average TV ad. They pack a lot into a short space. And they are there to do something: grip the imagination, help you see something in a new way, and act upon it.

But of course the parables were spoken at a particular time to a particular people and whilst it's true that most of them are rooted in ordinary, everyday life and work, it's the ordinary everyday life and work of first century Palestine under Roman occupation. Back then, if you wanted to make a joke about lack of trustworthiness, you probably wouldn't refer to ad-people but you might say, "I used to be a shepherd so you can trust every word I say." Which no one today would find funny or unusual. Mike bridges the gap. And more.

Indeed, this book does four things compellingly and joyously.

It brings fresh insight to the parables by retelling them in the way that Jesus might have in Britain today. Today, for example, Jesus wouldn't have used a Samaritan as an example of someone being kind to a mugged stranger. After all, today, in Britain at least, 'Samaritans' are known for being 'good' – they're a wise, kind listening ear to people who feel they can't go on any longer. So, Mike chooses a supporter from a football team notorious for the violence of its fans. Which one you think that is may depend on who you support.

Secondly, and separately, Mike helps us understand the original context of the parable – who Jesus was talking to, when it happened, including any pertinent historical or social information – and that helps us read the original parable afresh, and understand Jesus' overall ministry more deeply.

Thirdly, he includes the original parable so we can read it again with fresh eyes. Mike isn't pretending he tells a better story than Jesus or that his version has captured everything a parable might have to say – there's often so much, and some of them have been understood in many different ways. The original Bible text is the key for him. And, as he knows, also for us.

Fourthly, he salts the book with personal reflections and examples – warmly, wittily, vulnerably, poignantly. And he peppers it with challenging questions, and the space – literally – to think about how to respond to Jesus' teaching in the way we lead our lives, in the way we treat our neighbours, and in the way we relate to God.

But beyond all that, there's a spirit to this book: a sense of wonder about Christ, a quiet awe at who he is, and what he came to do, and a heartfelt yearning that anyone who reads this book – wherever they are in relationship with God – would know his love, his joy, him more deeply. Now. And forever.

Mark Greene
The London Institute for Contemporary Christianity

WIRED:
STORIES THAT PACK A PUNCH

PARABLE: SMALL STORY, BIG TRUTH

Most of us can recall an outstanding teacher from our schooldays.
A teacher with a passion for their subject and for us.
A teacher with great wisdom.
A teacher with a unique teaching style
A teacher that made us want to learn.
A teacher that left an indelible mark on our lives.

Jesus was all this and more.
A brilliant teacher, who also happened to be the Son of God.
A teacher in whom two worlds intersected.
The spiritual and the physical.
Heaven and earth.

At the heart of his teaching lie the parables.
Stories that he created and related in his own words.
Stories that he told to reconcile his two perspectives.
Stories that use familiar, everyday settings to convey eternal, spiritual themes.
Stories that we can understand and from which we can learn life-changing truths.

Parable: earthly setting,
spiritual meaning

To spend time with the parables is to spend time with Jesus, with his disciples, with the crowds that followed him, and even with the authorities that opposed him.

To spend time with the parables enables us to see and engage with the spiritual themes that permeate the events, relationships and situations in our everyday lives.

The lives that we are living, here and today.

REWIRED:
WHEN IS A TABLET NOT A TABLET?

Tablet 30AD

Tablet 2020AD

Jesus was passionate about getting his message across.

We can see his frustration as even his closest followers struggled to get it:

'You of little faith, why are you talking among yourselves about having no bread? Do you still not understand.... How is it you don't understand that I was not talking to you about bread?' (Matthew 16: 8,9,11)

So, he used props and storylines drawn from everyday life.

Things that were culturally relevant.

Stories that true faith-seekers could understand and relate to.

Which begs a question.

If Jesus were telling these stories to you and me today, here and now, would he not realise that we are unfamiliar with the way of life in a first century, middle-eastern agricultural society?

Of course, he would. So, surely, he would create and relate stories rooted in our 21st century Western culture?

He would draw upon modern-day commerce, entertainment, media, technology, sport, medicine, social protocols.

And he would use them as physical, everyday analogies and storylines to communicate his eternal, spiritual themes.

He would keep the themes and messaging of the stories unchanged.

But he would wire his words into today's world.

This thought first struck me in the closing years of the last century.

It gave birth to the story of the 'Compassionate Millwall fan'.

One Sunday I preached from it.

People told me that it worked well, and they encouraged me to write more.

So, I did, and these led to a short sermon series.

After which, I could feel God nudging me to write still more.

Eventually, I realised he was nudging me to rewire all the parables.

I resisted the nudge. I didn't have the time. I had too many marketing consultancy projects. And a family. And I was training for marathons.

Plus, it was an intimidating challenge. There are a lot of parables.

But the nudge became an increasingly more forceful shove.

God simply shut down my marketing projects.

My wife and I became empty nesters.

And I realised that I would not better my 3h 43m marathon in Chicago.

So, eventually, I capitulated and sat down at my keyboard.

I developed a method of working.

My first task was to identify the main message that Jesus was seeking to communicate.

That had to be respected and protected. At all costs.

I've submitted my work to theologians to check that I have achieved this. They say I have. I pray that they are right.

But the parables often contain sub-themes, which I suspect was not Jesus' main thrust or even intent, but which as so often is the case in storytelling, grew unbidden out of the storyline. I also set out to identify these and, where possible, bring them out in my retelling.

I think I've been reasonably successful, but not universally so. Sometimes it has proved impossible to entirely replicate all the first century cultural analogies.

On the other hand, some sub-themes have emerged from my own story-telling. Where I am conscious that this is the case I have checked them against Jesus' teaching elsewhere. If they have stood scrutiny I have let them remain.

For instance, you'll see that I have used a ski slope white-out in my retelling of the Lost Sheep. When I told the story at my church a keen skier said she was transfixed by the concept. In a white-out, she said, you feel isolated, afraid and terribly alone. The retelling had helped her see the parable from the sheep's perspective, lost in a spiritual white-out.

I had not spotted this, and it's entirely likely that there are other 'sub-messages' that I have not spotted. As you read these stories they may speak a message peculiar to you and you alone. If so, listen hard, because it's not from me: it's God speaking directly to you.

Finally, and crucially, I must stress that I have rewired the parables to supplement the originals, not to replace them.

Which is why I have also included the stories as Jesus himself told them.

I happily acknowledge that Jesus was a far better storyteller than me!

HOTWIRED:
INSTRUCTIONS FOR USE

[If you're a bloke, you may be thinking of skipping this bit. Don't!]

This is a resource book.

When you read it make sure you have a pen in your hand.

And use it, liberally.

Cross out what you don't agree with.

Underline what you do. Amend. Annotate.

Don't feel a need to read the whole book at one go. Take your time. Take as much time to read it as it has taken me to write it. Hint: that's a lot of time. As you read, have a cup of tea or coffee. By yourself. Then maybe discuss it over a glass of wine with some friends. That's very biblical. What the original hearers may have done.

Each parable follows the same format:

RETELLING

As I've said, the themes and messaging of the parables are timeless.

But the storylines are time-limited.

The product is terrific; but the packaging is perhaps a little dated.

Imagine a world without teabags. Or without squeezable honey, mayonnaise, Marmite. A world of hard unspreadable butter; milk only in glass bottles.

You might be saying: 'Oh, yes please' in which case you may like this....

REMINDING

After each retelling I've included the original parable. It's in the NIV translation: sorry if that's not your bag. There's always Bible Gateway!

Resetting and retelling happen a lot. Like the excellent BBC series: 'Chaucer retold'. Or Joe Cocker's cover of *With a little help from my friends*. Or the remake of The Italian Job.

I'm a Shakespeare junkie. Consequently, I've seen many productions that reset his plays in a modern setting. Often, they add fresh angles, which expand and enrich my experience. But invariably I find myself cross-referring back to the original text. It's great to hold the two in tension.

Another reason why I've included the original parables.

INTERPRETATION

Occasionally the Gospels show Jesus having to explain his parables to his audience. Given that the audience who didn't get it often included the people who wrote or inspired the Gospels, I'm suspecting that Jesus had to explain his stories more times than they cared to record!

Which brought me to the tricky bit.

My original intention was to just rewire the story and let the audience take it from there. But, my friends urged me not to do that. They said it would be a complete cop-out.

They pushed me to draw out some messaging and implications.

I'm not ordained and have not had formal theological training. (Neither did Jesus, but he did have the advantage of being the Son of God). So, look on my thoughts as a starter for ten. If they are helpful, great – build on them. If they're not, please feel free to ignore them.

But, either way, do take time to think what the parable (original, rewired, or I strongly suggest, the two together) may be saying to you.

REFLECTION

Jesus was the consummate teacher. When he wasn't telling stories, he was asking questions.

I like both approaches.

So, I've also posed some questions which I've had the temerity to upgrade and call 'Reflections'.

RESPONSE

This is always a blank page as I have nothing to say here.

Because this is all about you.

And what you think and say is as important as anything I've written in this book.

As an author, I know how intimidating a blank page can be. But I encourage you to try and write something, anything.

Look at it as a letter to Jesus.

That's what I did and look at where it has led me...

WHERE TO START?

Many authors say that the first page is the most difficult. That their brain suddenly becomes as blank as the page or screen.

But that's about *how* to start and that wasn't my problem. I was presented with umpteen parables to be getting on with. Potential storylines were firing my brain, not freezing it.

No, my problem was *where* to start: which parable should be first up and what should be the order thereafter.

In my first draft, I decided to take things in biblical order: start with the parables recorded by Matthew; then onto Mark; and finally sweep up with Luke. (John wasn't big on parables!)

Then I was struck by a 'Big Idea'. How about putting them into chronological order?

Great idea.

Bad idea.

I rapidly discovered that biblical chronology is fraught with 'challenges'. I knew that was the case with the Old Testament, but surely the New Testament would be a lot easier, particularly the Gospels. Nope. For instance, I discovered that John's Gospel is the only one that makes it clear that Jesus' ministry spanned 3 years; Matthew, Mark and Luke were more concerned with recording what happened, rather than when and in what order.

So, there are mismatches within and across the Gospels. Theologians of infinitely greater eminence than me have helpfully put forward varying suggestions on sequencing, which then, unhelpfully, differ.

It became clear to me that coming up with a chronology of Jesus' ministry and then inserting the parables within that was the theological equivalent of the search for the Holy Grail. But, like Lancelot and Indiana Jones, I persevered. My research threw up several interpretations. All I had to do was choose one. But which?

There was one that stood out, because it listed the first parable to be told as 'new wine into old wineskins'; and the last as 'sheep and goats'. This meant that Jesus' first parable was about wine and told at the same time as his first miracle at the wedding in Cana. Which was also all about wine. And both the parable and the miracle presaged the beginning of his ministry. That worked for me. It also meant that his last parable was about his second coming and Judgement Day. That also worked for me.

In fact, I became incredibly excited because I was seeing the parables in a new way: in the light of Jesus' ministry.

I was initially surprised to find a year's gap between the first and second parables. But then I realised that, during that time, Jesus was finding his feet and gathering his disciples. So, the second and third parables, the lamp under the bushel, and the wise and foolish builders, came as the culmination to his first major teaching session, the Sermon on the Mount; and formed a powerful injunction to his new adherents to pay heed to what he had said.

The 'Heaven is' series of parables accompanies the sending out of the disciples on their preaching mission and, in effect, says: 'Here's the message I want you to put across'.

Then Jesus told lots of stories on his journey to Jerusalem (there may have been one, two or three such journeys, depending on how one interprets the various Gospel storylines.) I like to think of these journeys as the biblical precursor to the 'Canterbury Tales'.

And, finally, the 'Meek, mild as if' and the 'Where do you stand?' series were told during what we now know as Holy Week.

My chronological ordering effort was well worth it because when I looked at the parables again in this context of Jesus' ministry it added a considerable amount of extra meaning. So much so, that I had to re-write several interpretations to accommodate the new insights.

This is how I answered the question: 'Where to start?' (and indeed, 'where to follow and end?'). I do not claim 100% accuracy for the chronology. In fact, your guess is probably as good as mine.

But, hey, this is my book so we're going to go with mine.

However, just because I've written them in this order doesn't mean you have to read them that way. Feel free to pick and mix. After all, it's now *your* book.

CHRONOLOGY

Timeline of Jesus' Ministry

AD 26

Summer	Baptism
	Wilderness temptations
Autumn	First miracle:

AD 27

Winter	Cleansing of the temple
	Woman at the well
Summer	Andrew, Peter,
	James & John join
Autumn	Matthew joins

AD 28

Winter	Jesus chooses the 12 disciples
Spring	Sermon on the Mount
Summer	Travel through Galilee
Autumn	Calming of storm; disciples sent out

AD 29

Winter	Feeding of the 5000
Spring	Walk on water
Summer	Transfiguration
Autumn	Raising of Lazarus

AD 30

Winter	Journey to Jerusalem
	Healing of blind Bartimaeus
Spring	Visit to Martha & Mary
	Palm Sunday
	Cleansing of the temple
	Last Supper, arrest & crucifixion
	Resurrection

Timeline of the Parables

No 1:	New cloth & new wine water into wine
Nos 2–3:	Lamp under bushel > Wise & foolish builders
Nos 4–9:	Debtors & creditor > Sower
Nos 10–17:	'Heaven is' series
Nos 18–19:	Master & servant > Unmerciful servant
Nos 20–21:	Good Samaritan > Friend in need
Nos 22–24:	Places of honour > Counting the cost
Nos 25–27:	'Lost & found' series
Nos 28–33:	Shrewd steward >Talents
Nos 34–36:	'Meek, mild, as if' series
Nos 37–39:	'Where do you stand?' series

THE PARABLES

Rewired	Original
When new into old won't go	New cloth and new wine
The Angel and the Ferrari	Lamp under the bushel
The astute and reckless investors	Wise and foolish builders
The two punters	Debtors and creditor
The selfish lawyer	Rich fool
The night watch	Alert servants
The CEO's dilemma	Faithful steward
The failing project	Fig tree without figs
The reluctant advertiser	Sower
Heaven is...	
Junk mail	Weeds
The pension fund	Growing seed
Look up and look in	Mustard seed and the yeast
The penny and the carp	Hidden treasure and the pearl
The job applications	Net
The wine merchant	Owner of the house
...Heaven is	
The two drivers	Master and his servant
The vindictive landlord	Unmerciful servant
The compassionate Millwall fan	Good Samaritan
The panicking colleague	Friend in need
A dramatic night at the Oscars	Places of honour at the wedding feast
The free lunch	Great banquet
The no-good do-gooders	Counting the cost
Lost (and found)	
The missing pupil	Lost sheep
The lost wedding ring	Lost coin
The tale of the teenage wastrel	Prodigal son
(Lost) and found	
The sassy theme park manager	Shrewd steward
The two landlords	Rich man and Lazarus
The labourers on the building site	Workers in the vineyard
The referee's tale	Persistent widow
Jousting on the hustings	Pharisee and the tax collector
The store managers	Talents
Meek, mild, as if...	
A tale of two plumbers	Two sons
The rebellious board	Tenants
The big match	Wedding banquet
...Meek, mild, as if	
Where do you stand?	
Tales of the expected	Fig tree
The impatient paparazzi	Ten virgins
A shanty of yachts and motorboats	Sheep and goats
Where do *you* stand?	

WHEN NEW INTO OLD WON'T GO

Two tales of when new into old won't go

Whilst Jesus was having a meal at Matthew's house, some of John the Baptist's followers came to ask him why he and his disciples did not follow the 'old rules' about fasting. As was his wont, Jesus replied with some stories and questions:

I took my car to the garage the other day.

It's an old Ford Cortina and I'm really fond of it. But the bodywork is now pretty shoddy, so I wanted to know whether they could source and fit another body shell.

'I could probably dig up a body shell somewhere,' the mechanic said, 'But the chassis is completely rusted, and no way will it support a new body shell. It would simply fall apart.'

'Well, OK, how about just fitting a new engine?' I replied, somewhat downcast, 'This one has done 400,000 miles.'

The mechanic laughed like a drain. 'I can certainly find you a new engine, but do you really want me to do that? If I put it in, the whole car will disintegrate the first time you drive it!

'What you need is a new engine with a new chassis and body shell. It will set you back a bit, but that way you'll still have your beloved Cortina, and it will be fit for future purpose.'

What would you guys have done?

The next day I called an electrician out to my house.

'I'd like you to install a state of the art electronic security system.'

'Yep, I could do that but why bother? Your fuse board isn't man enough:the system would be constantly tripping.'

'Well, in that case let's just fit a new consumer unit,' I replied, somewhat smugly, deploying the entirety of my limited electrical lexicon.

I received a pitying look. 'Do you really want me to do that? If I do, I'll need to re-wire the whole house as you'll have fuses popping faster than champagne corks at a wedding; that's if the house hasn't burnt down first.

'You need to re-wire, fit a new consumer unit and then install the security system. It won't be cheap, but it will make your house fit for future purpose.'

Again, what would you guys have done?

The parable of new cloth and new wine

Matthew 9:16-17

[16]*'No one sews a patch of unshrunk cloth on an old garment, for the patch will pull away from the garment, making the tear worse.* [17]*Neither do people pour new wine into old wineskins. If they do, the skins will burst; the wine will run out and the wineskins will be ruined. No, they pour new wine into new wineskins, and both are preserved.'*

Luke 5:36-38

[36]*He told them this parable:'No one tears a piece out of a new garment to patch an old one. Otherwise, they will have torn the new garment, and the patch from the new will not match the old.* [37]*And no one pours new wine into old wineskins. Otherwise, the new wine will burst the skins; the wine will run out and the wineskins will be ruined.* [38]*No, new wine must be poured into new wineskins.'*

Mark 2:21-22

[21]*'No one sews a patch of unshrunk cloth on an old garment. Otherwise, the new piece will pull away from the old, making the tear worse.* [22]*And no one pours new wine into old wineskins. Otherwise, the wine will burst the skins, and both the wine and the wineskins will be ruined. No, they pour new wine into new wineskins.'*

> *No one sews a patch of unshrunk cloth on an old garment*
> MATTHEW 9:16

So, what's this story saying to us, here and now?

This short and enigmatic story is Jesus' first parable, told at the very beginning of his ministry.

Around the same time, Jesus was also performing his first miracle at the wedding in Cana. So, in a perfect piece of divine symmetry, his first parable and his first miracle both involve wine; and both point towards the culmination of his ministry with the cup of wine at the Last Supper.

Nothing Jesus did or said was ever anything less than deeply significant.

In that vein, at the very outset of his ministry, Jesus told this parable to make the point that he had come to do new things in a new way; and that people should not expect him to be subject to, or conform to, old traditions.

Things they were a-changing.

As we all know, change can be an uncomfortable and threatening process; but it can also be exciting and revitalising.

The best way to deal with change is to approach it in the yet-to-be story of the future rather than closed-book history of the past. What and where is it leading to? What are the challenges and opportunities it will create?

As Jesus himself said:*'Do not think that I have come to abolish the Law or the Prophets; I have not come to abolish them but to fulfil them'* (Matt 5:17).

When we accept Jesus into our lives, he will change us.

Some of that change will be uncomfortable. But, if we embrace it, Jesus will change the whole of our character and our life for the better.

We shall emerge from the process not just as a renovation but as a completely new creation.

Fit for future purpose:and an eternal future at that.

Wow! Doesn't that leave us wanting to hear more stories?

Which is why Jesus told this as his first parable.

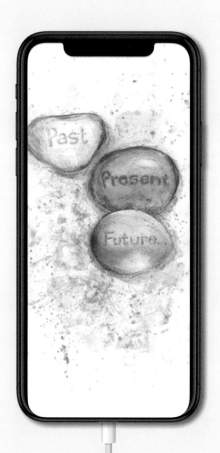

Am I fit for future purpose?

(How has Jesus changed me, and why?)

What is this story saying to me, here and now?

THE ANGEL AND THE FERRARI

Jesus' first recorded piece of extended preaching was the 'Sermon on the Mount', which starts with the 'Beatitudes': a series of eight blessings that set out the standards Jesus requires from us for spiritual living; together with the consequent benefits. (The rest of the sermon sets out how these spiritual standards should also shape our behaviours, and we'll explore this in the next parable.) At the end of the Beatitudes, Jesus issued a challenge to his followers, which naturally he couldn't resist illustrating with a story or two:

Your mission is to be an example to the world. Take it seriously...

When Antony Gormley had finished sculpting the Angel of the North, did Gateshead Council tuck it away in a small shopping centre?

No! They placed it on a hill overlooking the A1 and the mainline railway. Where all visitors could see it.

And when Ferrari launch a new model, do they invite a couple of local press journalists to a sandwich lunch in a back-street garage?

No! They build a massive and very glitzy stand at the Geneva Motor Show and fly in the world's media to see the car unveiled by a Hollywood superstar.

The parable of the lamp under the bushel

Matthew 5:14–16

[14]'*You are the light of the world. A town built on a hill cannot be hidden.* [15]*Neither do people light a lamp and put it under a bowl. Instead they put it on its stand, and it gives light to everyone in the house.* [16]*In the same way, let your light shine before others, that they may see your good deeds and glorify your Father in heaven.*'

You are the light of the world
MATTHEW 5:14

So, what's this story saying to us, here and now?

Centuries ago, Christianity dominated the arts scene in the Western world.

Music, art, poetry, architecture, sculpture:the vast majority of the classic works, were created to be in praise of God.

The Christian theme was a shining beacon. Churches were built on hills, with steeples and towers so they could be seen from miles around.

These days, Christian literature is confined to less than half an aisle in Waterstones; there are more famous paintings of cultural celebrities than biblical characters; and seldom does a Christian-themed song get airplay, let alone make the charts. Even at Christmas.

It's hard for us, individually, to do much about this.

But how visible are we, individually, as Christians? Yes, it's great that we go to church, but most of the rest of the world don't see us there.

6% of Brits are active Christians. Here's what they look like on a Sunday Morning:

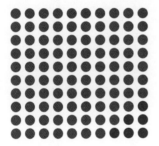

But, here's what they look like during the rest of the week.

So, the question for us, as individuals, is how do we make our faith, and Christ, visible to our families, neighbours, friends, colleagues and acquaintances. It's the challenge Jesus issued to his disciples, and it's the challenge he is issuing to you and me, here and now.

Come on Jesus light
my fire!

What is this story saying to me, here and now?

THE ASTUTE AND RECKLESS INVESTORS

To conclude the Sermon on the Mount, Jesus told this parable to emphasise how important it was that people acted upon what he was saying:

The late 1980s was an incredible time to be working in the City. This was the time of yuppy-mania:young guns toting the new-fangled mobile phones, tearing around in the latest Porsche turbo and making five or six-figure bonuses.

At the end of 1988, two such types – Hamza and Wei – each picked up a £150,000 year-end bonus. Neither needed a new Ferrari; each decided that their 45ft powerboat was big enough; and both had taken two Caribbean holidays that year. But whilst they obviously qualified as conspicuous consumers they were also savvy enough to realise that the good times might not run forever. They each therefore decided to invest their latest windfalls to provide greater security in the longer-term. Each decided he would buy a business.

But what?

Hamza, always impetuous, was typically quick off the mark. He was clear about the sort of business he wanted to buy. It needed to satisfy two criteria. First, it had to be something which he would personally get excited about – fashion and glamour being top of the list. Second, it had to provide a quick return on his investment. He found exactly what he was after in the form of a Porsche dealership. He quickly did the deal – not even bothering to negotiate down the sale price (even though, at half a million pounds, it was more than three times his original intended investment).

Wei also had just two criteria. But he showed himself to be more cautious and, arguably, a little cannier than Hamza. For him, a 'glamour product' and big short-term rewards were not the issues. The business he was after would need to display a sound business model and offer long-term growth potential. He identified three companies, did extensive due diligence on each, and eventually bought a small chain of shops selling budget-priced DIY materials.

For a while, all was fine. Wei's discount DIY chain did steady business; Hamza's Porsche importing dealership boomed.

Then the situation changed. High interest rates and poor exchange rates led to increases in the costs of bought-in goods – especially imports. Wage demands started to spiral. And finally, real disaster struck as the chill wind of recession blew throughout the country, but with its most severe impact in the high-rolling City. Hamza's business crashed as he found himself with large stocks of expensive Porsches with no-one to buy them and half a dozen high-salaried salesmen demanding to be 'looked after' one way or another. The arithmetic simply wouldn't work and the whole show collapsed around him, leaving him owing hundreds of thousands of pounds. With no job in the City (he'd been made redundant himself) he was forced to declare himself bankrupt.

Wei had also been made redundant from his City job. But the homework he'd done on his business investment now paid off. His business plan provided a firm foundation in these more challenging times. The demand for reasonably-priced DIY materials held up as people put off moving home and did up their current ones instead. His staff accepted a pay freeze linked to a promise of catch-up bonuses as and when things improved. The basic economics and cashflow of his business was sound. He found that it grew through this period of adversity. He gave his friend Hamza a job as a delivery driver. Over time, he was able to reward his staff and expand the business. It went from strength to strength and his small DIY chain is now a large nationwide concern. And Hamza is his Transport and Logistics Director.

The parable of the wise and foolish builders

Matthew 7:24-29

24'Therefore everyone who hears these words of mine and puts them into practice is like a wise man who built his house on the rock. 25The rain came down, the streams rose, and the winds blew and beat against that house; yet it did not fall, because it had its foundation on the rock. 26But everyone who hears these words of mine and does not put them into practice is like a foolish man who built his house on sand. 27The rain came down, the streams rose, and the winds blew and beat against that house, and it fell with a great crash.' 28 When Jesus had finished saying these things, the crowds were amazed at his teaching, 29because he taught as one who had authority, and not as their teachers of the law.

Luke 6:47-49

47 'As for everyone who comes to me and hears my words and puts them into practice, I will show you what they are like. 48 They are like a man building a house, who dug down deep and laid the foundation on rock. When the flood came, the torrent struck that house but could not shake it, because it was well built. 49 But the one who hears my words and does not put them into practice is like a man who built a house on the ground without a foundation. The moment the torrent struck that house, it collapsed and its destruction was complete.'

Therefore everyone who hears these words of mine and puts them into practice is like a wise man who built his house on the rock
MATTHEW 7:24

So, what's this story saying to us, here and now?

Jesus original parable is almost self-evident. What builder wouldn't build on solid ground? It's obvious, isn't it?

So, it may be helpful to think about why Jesus told the parable.

As I've pointed out, it comes as the concluding element of the Sermon on the Mount:Jesus' first great teaching exposition. It's a long sermon occupying three chapters of Matthew's Gospel, and it's well worth reading through in one go.

The Sermon is very challenging as Jesus tells it to call people to a higher standard of moral and ethical living. So high that many scholars have dismissed it as being unrealistic. Others argue that that is the very point:the only way we can get anywhere near these standards is with the help of Jesus.

All of which makes this parable really important, because Jesus uses it as a call to us to base our lives on his words, his teaching. A call to action. The people who heard it at the time were amazed at the authority with which he spoke. Unlike the prevaricating teachers of the law, Jesus was a man who dealt in certainties. (Being the Son of God helped in this respect!)

But the point remains that our reaction to the parable may well be:'Why on earth wouldn't a builder put his house on rock?'

But that's so often the way with Jesus' words and teaching. When we read it, it seems absolutely unarguable. The trouble comes when we try to put it into practice. It's not easy. In fact, it's really, really, difficult. The temptation then is to shift bits of that teaching onto some sandy ground that may be a bit easier. (In Hamza's case, into a business that produces a faster buck, albeit with higher risk.)

And we may also have the serpent hissing into our ear:'Did Jesus really say…?'

Even with Jesus helping us, it can be a struggle. Without him it's impossible.

So, this is mainly a parable about faith. Building our faith upon the rock that is Jesus. Putting our complete and absolute trust in him.

What do I want to
build on my rock?

What is this story saying to me, here and now?

A TALE OF TWO PUNTERS

Jesus looked at the man before him: 'I'm going to tell you a story.'

'Well, if you insist,' came the reply.

'Yes, I do'.

Linda and Valerie worked as nurses in their local hospice.

They would be the first to admit that the pay wasn't great, but they were able to get by. And, like many hospice nurses, they saw it as a vocation as much as a job.

But it was emotionally demanding, so whenever they could afford it, they made a point of taking a City Break holiday: an escapist sightseeing and shopping combo. Over the years they had 'done' Venice, Rome, New York, Edinburgh, and Paris.

This time they had come to Las Vegas for a long weekend.

Checking into their rooms at one of the big hotels on the strip ('cheap as chips rates', Linda had observed when they made their booking) they headed out to see the sights and check out the shops. They would also call into the casinos but restrict themselves to a spectating role.

Sunday night saw them back in their hotel. They were due to check out early the next day.

After dinner, they went into the casino to do some more 'punter-watching'. But this time they decided that they couldn't really go to Las Vegas and not have a flutter.

So, they went their separate ways. Linda to roulette; Valerie to blackjack.

At 8am the next morning they met up at the check-out desk.

Valerie gasped when she saw her bill.

'$4,500! There's a huge mistake here, surely.' The cashier checked the details. 'Nope it's correct, honey. You were in the casino last night and bought $3,000 worth of chips on your room account.'

'But I only ordered $300 worth,' exclaimed Valerie.

'I'm sorry, sweetheart. The system never gets it wrong.'

Valerie turned to Linda 'What on earth am I going to do? There's no way I can pay this.'

But Linda was as white as a ghost, a sheet of paper held in her trembling fingers.

'Oh no, you haven't made the same mistake have you,'

Linda couldn't speak, couldn't even breathe.

Valerie grabbed the paper from her and her face turned puce.

'$45,000,' she shrieked. 'That's more than a year's pay. Oh, what a nightmare.'

The two girls looked at each other and burst into tears, hysterical.

A security guy appeared. 'You'd better come with me ladies.'

He led them into an office and left the room.

The two girls sat there, sobbing uncontrollably.

The door opened, and a smartly-dressed man came in and sat down on the other side of the desk.

'I'm the Casino Manager and it seems you two have been somewhat foolish.'

There was no answer.

The man looked at the papers on his desk.

'It says here you both work as nurses at a hospice, so I'm guessing there's no way you're able to pay.'

Again, there was no answer.

'My Mom and my Pop died in a hospice. Cancer took them both within 12 months. But they died well. The hospice nurses were terrific'

He paused and looked at the sobbing girls. Then he ripped up the papers and dropped the pieces in the waste bin.

'Have this one on us. But just don't ever be so stupid again.'

Jesus' eyes bore into those of the young man.

'Answer me this: who would have been the more thankful, Valerie or Linda?'

'I guess Linda, as her bill was 10 times as big.'

'Exactly,' said Jesus.

The parable of the debtors and creditor

Luke 7:36–50

³⁶ When one of the Pharisees invited Jesus to have dinner with him, he went to the Pharisee's house and reclined at the table. ³⁷ A woman in that town who lived a sinful life learned that Jesus was eating at the Pharisee's house, so she came there with an alabaster jar of perfume. 38 As she stood behind him at his feet weeping, she began to wet his feet with her tears. Then she wiped them with her hair, kissed them and poured perfume on them.

³⁹ When the Pharisee who had invited him saw this, he said to himself, 'If this man were a prophet, he would know who is touching him and what kind of woman she is – that she is a sinner.'

⁴⁰ Jesus answered him, 'Simon, I have something to tell you.'

'Tell me, teacher,' he said.

⁴¹ 'Two people owed money to a certain moneylender. One owed him five hundred denarii, and the other fifty. ⁴² Neither of them had the money to pay him back, so he forgave the debts of both. Now which of them will love him more?'

⁴³ Simon replied, 'I suppose the one who had the bigger debt forgiven.'

'You have judged correctly,' Jesus said.

⁴⁴ Then he turned towards the woman and said to Simon, 'Do you see this woman? I came into your house. You did not give me any water for my feet, but she wet my feet with her tears and wiped them with her hair. ⁴⁵ You did not give me a kiss, but this woman, from the time I entered, has not stopped kissing my feet. ⁴⁶ You did not put oil on my head, but she has poured perfume on my feet. ⁴⁷ Therefore, I tell you, her many sins have been forgiven – as her great love has shown. But whoever has been forgiven little loves little.'

⁴⁸ Then Jesus said to her, 'Your sins are forgiven.'

⁴⁹ The other guests began to say among themselves, 'Who is this who even forgives sins?'

⁵⁰ Jesus said to the woman, 'Your faith has saved you; go in peace.'

> Then Jesus said to her, 'Your sins are forgiven
> LUKE 7:48

So, what's this story saying to us, here and now?

I've included the whole of the original passage as I think it is important to read this parable in the context in which it was originally told. (That holds true for most of the parables, but particularly so in this case.)

I must confess that I frequently catch myself being more than somewhat self-righteous. *'Yes, I know I need forgiveness – after all none of us is perfect. But I haven't got too much wrong, have I? If only I was a bigger sinner I'd be able to confess more easily.'*

And sometimes I even catch myself thinking of someone else:a real 'wrong'un'. I then tell myself that I may need forgiving, but not THAT much, thank goodness.

Apart from being overly judgmental (a sin) I am of course completely wrong. As I am reminded every time I take communion and ask for forgiveness for the wrong things I have done in thought, word and deed; and the good things I have not done.

(How long do you have Lord?)

But, even if I were as good as my deluded thoughts try to persuade me I am, it wouldn't necessarily be an entirely good thing. I may actually be missing out.

A small crime requires small forgiveness; a large crime requires great forgiveness.

My middle daughter, Felicity, was – still is – terribly accident prone. When she was little we learned to fear the exclamation 'oops!' Generally, it would be just another glass broken, but not always. One of her greatest misdemeanours was dropping the bottle of vintage port we had saved from our wedding year with a view to opening it at our silver wedding.

Of course, it had been an accident, not a thing done with purpose or intent. And her remorse, contrition and tears were so intense that I couldn't do anything other than forgive. And I subsequently realised that was one of the times I loved her most.

Why should God be any different?

Plus, if we have been forgiven a lot, we know how real gratitude feels and that helps us show forgiveness and compassion to others.

The greater the forgiveness we have received, the greater our propensity and capability to fulfil our obligation to love and forgive others, unconditionally.

I think that's the point this parable makes.

REFLECTION AND PRAYER

Have mercy on me,
a sinner

What is this story saying to me, here and now?

THE SELFISH LAWYER

Jesus was asked to pronounce upon a family squabble. As is so often the case, material possessions lay at the heart of it. He politely refused to become embroiled in the spat and instead told this parable:

Enter GL54 8VE into your SatNav and it will take you 90 miles due west out of London along the M4, then north onto the A429 and finally – via a series of increasingly unmetalled and grass-adorned minor roads – to Little Ditching.

But the trip will have been worth it, for Little Ditching is a wonderfully picturesque Cotswold village, star turn of countless greetings cards and biscuit tins.

Amazingly it has escaped the clutches of the weekend retreat market and remains home to a close-knit indigenous community. Central to their social whirl is, of course, the local pub together with an exceptionally well-equipped village hall.

Which has a story to tell.

It starts 20 years ago when the hall was not so well equipped. To be accurate, it was in terminal decay. A structural survey had diagnosed rising damp and subsidence. It had also recommended complete re-wiring and re-roofing, concluding with a refurbishment estimate of £270,000 – well beyond the means of the village community. The hall had no architectural or historical provenance and so no grants would be forthcoming. Even though it was home to the local guides, scouts, WI, amateur dramatic society and numerous other societies, it contravened just about every Health and Safety regulation going. And so, the village steeled itself for its inevitable closure and probable demolition.

One of the more recently arrived residents was a 50-year-old commercial lawyer who had used a year-end bonus and an unexpected bequest from a distant relative to fund his early retirement. But soon after his arrival in the village he had a second stroke of good fortune. And this time it truly was a fortune: a £19m lottery win.

Having not bothered to tick the 'no publicity' box, he was soon beset with approaches from any number of good causes. He did not in any way find this a problem, having decided from the outset that good causes didn't come any better than himself!

A long-time admirer of modern art, he was soon a familiar figure in Mayfair's best galleries and auction houses. Fascination turned to obsession. He converted his basement into a private display area. Obsession turned to perversion. This was his collection:for his eyes only. Every night he would retreat to his gallery, pour himself a large scotch – or several – and suffuse himself in self-content.

When Health and Safety officials forced the immediate closure of the village hall, he unexpectedly contacted the Town Clerk with an offer of help. Great rejoicing all round quickly soured when it became apparent that his idea of help was to acquire the hall (at a knock-down price) and convert it into a private gallery (for his use only) for his art collection which by now had outgrown his basement. The council, realising they had no other options, reluctantly accepted his offer.

And a no-expense-spared makeover saw the hall immaculately restored. The roof renewed. Foundations underpinned, a mezzanine floor added and air-conditioning throughout.

The art collection was transferred, more pieces acquired, and a set of six sculptures especially commissioned for the re-opening ceremony. An opening to which a grand total of one person was invited:himself. After all this was a private gallery, the public could go whistle.

The day before the opening he could hardly contain himself. As the day wore on, his nervous excitement triggered a migraine. Determined not to let this spoil the occasion, he retired to bed with aspirin and a very large scotch.

Two months later, the Parish Council re-acquired the hall for the same price they had sold it.

The art collection was in the hands of a leading auctioneer.

And the man was in a nursing home.

The stroke he suffered that night had spared his life, but left him paralysed – and blind.

The parable of the rich fool

Luke 12:13–21

¹³ *Some one in the crowd said to him, 'Teacher, tell my brother to divide the inheritance with me.'*

¹⁴ *Jesus replied, 'Man, who appointed me a judge or an arbiter between you?'* ¹⁵ *Then he said to them, 'Watch out! Be on your guard against all kinds of greed; life does not consist in an abundance of possessions.'*

¹⁶ *And he told them this parable: 'The ground of a certain rich man yielded an abundant harvest.* ¹⁷ *He thought to himself, "What shall I do? I have no place to store my crops."*

¹⁸ *Then he said, "This is what I'll do. I will tear down my barns and build bigger ones, and there I will store my surplus grain.* ¹⁹ *And I'll say to myself, 'You have plenty of grain laid up for many years. Take life easy; eat, drink and be merry.'"*

²⁰ *'But God said to him, "You fool! This very night your life will be demanded from you. Then who will get what you have prepared for yourself?"*

²¹ *'This is how it will be with whoever stores up things for themselves but is not rich towards God.'*

> *This is how it will be with whoever stores up things for themselves but is not rich towards God*
>
> LUKE 12:21

So, what's this story saying to us, here and now?

A dramatic tale. Chilling even. And certainly tragic.

But, like all the parables, told to drive home a simple message.

In this case:live life generously.

God longs to bless our lives.

Sometimes we may feel (wrongly) that we have 'earned' that blessing.

At other times, it just seems to drop into our laps.

Most of us will have experienced both types of blessing on our lives.

The commercial lawyer had clearly worked hard at his job, sufficiently so to achieve success and a bumper bonus by the age of 50. Rewards well-earned. On the other hand, the lottery win was completely fortuitous.

The rich farmer in the original parable would probably have worked hard to make his money. The bumper harvest was unexpected icing on the cake.

Either way, both were richly blessed.

Jesus is not saying that you should not enjoy your blessings. But he is saying that how you enjoy them is important.

If someone does us a great favour, our natural instinct is to look to pay them back somehow.

But God doesn't want us to pay his blessings back. He wants us to pay them forward.

Blessings are not given to us solely for our own benefit. We should always look to share our blessings:to use them to bless other people.

There's also a very important sub-plot in this parable regarding our attitude to our possessions. Are they serving us or are we serving them? Are they just objects or have they become objects of worship? If, for any reason, God were to ask us, would we be prepared to let them go?

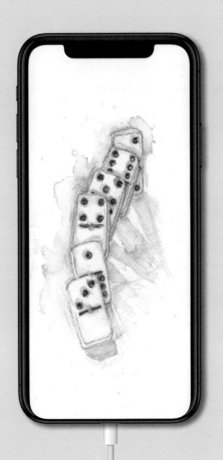

Am I living my life
generously?

What is this story saying to me, here and now?

THE STORY OF THE NIGHT WATCH

Jesus told this story to stress to his disciples the importance of them maintaining their spiritual alertness:

Faces glowed ghostly white in the darkness as light snow drifted down.

B Platoon were on a night exercise in Wiltshire.

Their mission: to hold a 'gun emplacement' against a suspected 'enemy attack'.

Lieutenant Jenkins was in charge; her Captain having been summoned to a staff meeting at HQ an hour ago.

Watch-keeping was being done in pairs, each stretch just an hour long to maintain maximum alertness.

The snow became heavier, and it lay like a winter duvet, muffling and deadening sound.

The hours passed.

Suddenly a noise. In reality, a snow-laden twig being broken; but it broke the eerie silence like a pistol shot.

The sentry whipped around and levelled his rifle:'Halt and identity yourself.'

'Winchester Cathedral' came the reply:the pass-code for that night.

'Advance.'

The figure of Captain McIntyre resolved itself.

'Well done lad. It's nearly dawn, so you can stand down. Give me your rifle and I'll take the next spell.'

'Thank you, Sir. It really challenges your attention doesn't it, not knowing when things are going to happen?'

'Too right, son,' replied his Captain. 'You can never afford to let your guard down, no matter who you are. In 1944, if Rommel had anticipated the invasion, our boys would never have got off the beaches.'

'Always expect the unexpected, that's my motto.'

The parable of the alert servants

Luke 12:35–40

[35] 'Be dressed ready for service and keep your lamps burning, [36] like servants waiting for their master to return from a wedding banquet, so that when he comes and knocks they can immediately open the door for him. [37] It will be good for those servants whose master finds them watching when he comes. Truly I tell you, he will dress himself to serve, will have them recline at the table and will come and wait on them. [38] It will be good for those servants whose master finds them ready, even if he comes in the middle of the night or toward daybreak. [39] But understand this: If the owner of the house had known at what hour the thief was coming, he would not have let his house be broken into. [40] You also must be ready, because the Son of Man will come at an hour when you do not expect him.'

"

You also must be ready, because the Son of Man will come at an hour when you do not expect him
LUKE 12:40

So, what's this story saying to us, here and now?

'Always expect the unexpected' was Captain McIntyre's motto.

Not unexpectedly, it's the sort of thing you'd expect to hear from a soldier.

Unexpected things, good and bad, happen to us pretty frequently:a premium bond win, a puncture, a surprise call from a friend, a power cut. In fact, life is full of surprises.

Unexpected things that we are not expecting.

But, what unexpected news and occurrences should we be expecting?

How about prophecies? And miracles?

Nah, they don't happen now do they?

Are we sure?

When was the last time you heard a word from God?

Have you ever heard one?

If you have, the chances are it was whilst reading the Bible, or during a service, or in conversation with a Christian friend, or in a time of prayer and contemplation. Either then or shortly after.

And the chances are that the same applies for the last time God intervened in your life:to remove or ease a problem; or create an opportunity.

Prophecies and miracles are unexpected occurrences; they don't come to order.

But we should nevertheless expect them to happen.

And we can express that expectation through consistent, purposeful, anticipatory prayer.

God's word to us and his hand on our life tend to come unexpectedly.

But that doesn't mean we shouldn't expect it.

Even if we do. Or don't.

'Always expect the unexpected.'

How great are my expectations?

(Speak into and act in my life Lord)

What is this story saying to me, here and now?

THE TALE OF THE CEO'S DILEMMA

When Jesus had finished telling the story of the Alert Servants (*see:Night Watch*), Peter was keen to know whether it was meant for them, the disciples, or for everyone. Typically, Jesus' response took the form of another story:

Ebony Brydon was in a quandary.

As CEO of Time and Space Enterprises, she was responsible for delivering the 3-year Strategic Plan and the Annual Operating Profits.

That wasn't her quandary. She could do that falling off a log backwards. And had done for the past seven years. (Delivered the results that is, not fallen off a log.)

But, it is a truism that you can be a victim of your own success. And boy was that the case now.

The Board of TSE had been approached by a large American media company that was struggling to make the shift from print to video; from analogue to digital.

Under Ebony's guidance, TSE had managed to do just that, with considerable success. And now the US company wanted to shelter under the same umbrella; their shareholders had voted to merge with TSE, providing Ebony took the CEO role for the combined companies.

The TSE Board had bitten off the proffered, dollar-filled, hand.

So now Ebony had to relocate from London to New York.

But that wasn't her quandary either. She'd worked for 2 years in NYC earlier in her career and had no problem with returning. Quite the reverse, she loved the city.

No, her quandary was what to do with the management team at TSE in the UK.

She had two lieutenants.

Ernie Mountjoy ran the organisation's print assets:magazines and newspapers that had successfully managed the analogue to digital transition and still delivered a reasonable, but declining, part of the group's profit. Instinctively protective of his people and reluctant to take fast decisions, Ernie Mountjoy had been re-christened 'Erm'.

Then there was Mitch Miller. The boss of the rapidly growing broadcast and video division. Never one to shy away from a difficult decision he was commonly known as 'M2'. The fast, relentless and ruthless route to success.

With Ebony in day-to-day control it had all worked out just fine. A perfect cocktail of management. But now that Ebony was off to NYC the cherry was leaving the glass.

Her fear was that, in her absence, they would live up to their nicknames. That Erm would be overly protective of his declining republic and M2 would be overly ruthless in building his expanding empire.

But it was far, far worse than that.

Twelve months later Ebony extricated herself from the demands of the, now hugely successful, US business and spent a week in the UK assessing the business there:reviewing performance and scrutinising their plans for the year ahead.

She was both pleasantly surprised and totally horrified by what she found.

Pleasantly surprised because Erm's division had managed to grow its revenues and profits. Not hugely, but it far exceeded her expectations of a rapid decline.

She decided that Erm had proved his worth and would get a step up in the enlarged organisation.

But totally horrified because M2's division, of which she had expected so much, had imploded. Revenues down 30% and profits all but eradicated.

On closer examination, it became clear that Mitch had become a victim of his own publicity.

Long lunches and dinners with his cronies had over-ridden his judgment and alienated his producers and writers. Most of the creative talent had deserted to other broadcasters. Advertising monies had followed them. Unusually in an industry characterised by its 'luvviness', several long-serving and well-respected industry veterans told her exactly why they detested Mitch. 'Arrogant', 'drunk', 'over-bearing', 'calculatedly ruthless', 'insensitive' were frequent descriptors.

Interestingly, no-one accused him of being stupid. He was more than capable of running the business successfully but had lost the plot:led astray by his self-indulgence and undone by his anti-social demeanour.

There was a difficult conversation to be had.

'Mitch, you're fired with immediate effect. Clear your desk and go. Now. You knew what I wanted you to do. If I thought there was any doubt about that I would be more lenient. But you knew it and you ignored it. And as a result, other people suffered. Tell me if I'm wrong.'

And so, Mitch left. Not because he knew so little and did too much, but because he knew so much and yet did too little.

The parable of the faithful steward

Luke 12:41–48

[41] Peter asked, 'Lord, are you telling this parable to us, or to everyone?'

[42] The Lord answered, 'Who then is the faithful and wise manager, whom the master puts in charge of his servants to give them their food allowance at the proper time? [43] It will be good for that servant whom the master finds doing so when he returns. [44] Truly I tell you, he will put him in charge of all his possessions. [45] But suppose the servant says to himself, 'My master is taking a long time in coming,' and he then begins to beat the other servants, both men and women, and to eat and drink and get drunk. [46] The master of that servant will come on a day when he does not expect him and at an hour he is not aware of. He will cut him to pieces and assign him a place with the unbelievers.

[47] 'The servant who knows the master's will and does not get ready or does not do what the master wants will be beaten with many blows. [48] But the one who does not know and does things deserving punishment will be beaten with few blows. From everyone who has been given much, much will be demanded; and from the one who has been entrusted with much, much more will be asked.'

> *Lord, are you telling this parable to us, or to everyone?*
> **LUKE 12:41**

So, what's this story saying to us, here and now?

This parable packs a real punch.

Here it is in Jesus' own words:

'From everyone who has been given much, much will be demanded; and from the one who has been entrusted with much, much more will be asked.'

Here are a few facts about our world.

The richest 10% (anyone with financial and property assets worth more than £50,000) own 90% of the world's wealth.

The richest 1% own 50% of the world's wealth; the poorest 50% just 1%.

The richest 100 people in the world own as much as the poorest 3.5 billion.

World annual food production is 4 billion metric tonnes; enough to provide 6lbs of food each day for every one of the 7 billion humans on the planet.

But half of it, 2 billion metric tonnes, is wasted or thrown away.

The average American weighs 178 lbs; the average Asian 127lbs.

In the UK the average Body Mass Index is 27.0; in Ethiopia it's 20.3.

In Japan, life expectancy is 84 years; in Sierra Leone it's 46.

God has created a world with sufficient resources for all, but are we being faithful stewards of that world? True to God's original creative vision?

So, to repeat Peter's question:is this story being told to 'us' or everyone?

What do we think?

REFLECTION AND PRAYER

What's my worldview?

(And what is the world's view of me?)

What is this story saying to me, here and now?

THE FAILING PROJECT

All of us can be tempted to put off doing something difficult.

Like saying 'sorry' to someone.

Even to God.

Jesus urged his disciples not to procrastinate:

'Sorry, but I think it's time we pulled the plug on this one.'

The Chief Executive of the British Medical Institute was visiting their Research & Development centre in Cambridge.

'We've been working flat out on this vaccine for three years now and have got absolutely nowhere. We're wasting valuable resources that could be better used elsewhere, so I'm going to shut the project down.'

The project head, Dr Lyn Cooper, quickly interceded

'Sir, I can understand your frustration, but it's a vital project and I think we should give it one more push. I'll reshuffle the team and pull in some new faces. If we've still nothing to show this time next year then by all means close the project down.'

The parable of the fig tree without figs

Luke 13:1-9

Now there were some present at that time who told Jesus about the Galileans whose blood Pilate had mixed with their sacrifices. ²Jesus answered, 'Do you think that these Galileans were worse sinners than all the other Galileans because they suffered this way? ³I tell you, no! But unless you repent, you too will all perish. ⁴Or those eighteen who died when the tower in Siloam fell on them – do you think they were more guilty than all the others living in Jerusalem? ⁵I tell you, no! But unless you repent, you too will all perish.'

⁶Then he told this parable:'A man had a fig-tree growing in his vineyard, and he went to look for fruit on it but did not find any. ⁷So he said to the man who took care of the vineyard, "For three years now I've been coming to look for fruit on this fig-tree and haven't found any. Cut it down! Why should it use up the soil?"

⁸"'Sir," the man replied, "leave it alone for one more year, and I'll dig round it and fertilise it. ⁹If it bears fruit next year, fine! If not, then cut it down."'

> *If it bears fruit next year, fine! If not, then cut it down*
> LUKE 13:9

So, what's this story saying to us, here and now?

Jesus' ministry lasted for three years. The fig tree had been growing without fruit for three years.

A coincidence?

Speaking personally, I think not:Jesus was too purposeful a storyteller. I'm sure he used the three years deliberately.

So I've kept the same timescale in my rewiring .

Let's look at the context of the parable.

People were concerned about human rights atrocities and natural disasters. A repressive regime; a catastrophic accident. Not unlike the news bulletins of today.

But, in those days they weren't seen as accidents. They were regarded as acts of God, punishments:'Boy, those people must have been *really* bad. Lucky for us we're not as bad as them.'

'No, no, no,' says Jesus. 'You've got it all wrong. Those people were no better or worse than you. Unless you repent of your sins, *truly* repent of them, then in God's eyes, you're as bad as anyone else.'

This would have been truly shocking stuff for his audience.

And Jesus drives it home saying, in effect:'Look, despite all my teaching and preaching you're still not getting the message. Get your act together before it's too late.'

But, he sweetens the pill. The fig tree is given another year. Did it produce figs? Did the scientists create the vaccine?

Typically, a fig tree will not produce fruit until it is at least two years old. It can take up to six years. Big research projects do not provide instant results.

We're not told what happened. And that actually is not the point.

The point is that the extra time was given.

Cleverly, the parable does not let this stay of execution detract from the urgency of the message. Jesus will always give us more time, but anyone without Jesus in their life needs to bear in mind that, in this physical life, time is not infinite.

Footnote:After writing this last paragraph, I was struck by another thought. Many of us will be praying for a family member or a friend to come to Jesus. We may have been praying for years. And we should continue to pray, because Jesus doesn't really mind how long it takes someone to come to him; just as long as they do.

How long has my clock been ticking?

(Praise Jesus, the Lord of time)

What is this story saying to me, here and now?

THE RELUCTANT ADVERTISER

Jesus has been through a busy few days:travelling, teaching and healing many people, and clashing with the Pharisees. He tries to grab a bit of me-time on a lake shore but the crowds have continued to build and they find him. So, Jesus climbs into a boat, rows a short way off the shore and uses it as a platform to tell one of his most famous parables:

Emma Rossi had astounded her parents by painting her first watercolour landscape when just three years old. Twenty-two years later she had added seascapes to her repertoire and oils to her palette. Her portfolio was as extensive as her holiday travels, which covered four continents.

A friend persuaded her to turn her hobby into a business and so she rented a small shop in York and opened an art gallery.

At the end of her first week just two people had come inside:one to ask directions to the council offices, the other thinking that it was a new coffee shop.

That weekend she sought out her friend. 'Well I've gone for it as you advised, but I'm thinking it may have been a big mistake.'

'You should advertise the gallery,' came the suggestion. 'Don't be daft,' Emma replied, 'Everyone knows that's just a waste of money because it's expensive and people just ignore ads these days. So, I'm using social media.'

Her friend sucked her teeth. 'Hmm, social media? I'm not convinced that's going to work. You need to reach out way beyond your own social network. Yes, it's true that if you put an ad in the paper some people will not even notice it. And others will see it but ignore it. Still others will see it, be interested but then turn the page and forget it as something else grabs their attention. But there will also be those who will see it, be interested in it, remember it and act upon it. And they will give you a huge return on your investment. Trust me on this.'

And so, Emma emptied her bank account and bought a full-colour, double-page spread in the *Yorkshire Post*. Within two weeks she had sold three-quarters of her stock and received dozens of new commissions.

The parable of the sower

Matthew 13:1–9

That same day Jesus went out of the house and sat by the lake. [2] Such large crowds gathered around him that he got into a boat and sat in it, while all the people stood on the shore. [3] Then he told them many things in parables, saying: 'A farmer went out to sow his seed. [4] As he was scattering the seed, some fell along the path, and the birds came and ate it up. [5] Some fell on rocky places, where it did not have much soil. It sprang up quickly, because the soil was shallow. [6] But when the sun came up, the plants were scorched, and they withered because they had no root. [7] Other seed fell among thorns, which grew up and choked the plants. [8] Still other seed fell on good soil, where it produced a crop – a hundred, sixty or thirty times what was sown. [9] Whoever has ears, let them hear.'

Luke 8:4–8

[4] While a large crowd was gathering and people were coming to Jesus from town after town, he told this parable: [5] 'A farmer went out to sow his seed. As he was scattering the seed, some fell along the path; it was trampled on, and the birds ate it up. [6] Some fell on rocky ground, and when it came up, the plants withered because they had no moisture. [7] Other seed fell among thorns, which grew up with it and choked the plants. [8] Still other seed fell on good soil. It came up and yielded a crop, a hundred times more than was sown.' When he said this, he called out, 'Whoever has ears to hear, let them hear.'

Mark 4:1–9

Again Jesus began to teach by the lake. The crowd that gathered round him was so large that he got into a boat and sat in it out on the lake, while all the people were along the shore at the water's edge. [2] He taught them many things by parables, and in his teaching said: [3] 'Listen! A farmer went out to sow his seed. [4] As he was scattering the seed, some fell along the path, and the birds came and ate it up. [5] Some fell on rocky places, where it did not have much soil. It sprang up quickly, because the soil was shallow. [6] But when the sun came up, the plants were scorched, and they withered because they had no root. [7] Other seed fell among thorns, which grew up and choked the plants, so that they did not bear grain. [8] Still other seed fell on good soil. It came up, grew and produced a crop, some multiplying thirty, some sixty, some a hundred times.' [9] Then Jesus said, 'Whoever has ears to hear, let them hear.'

So, what's this story saying to us, here and now?

I love this parable! It's about the three S's: the Sower, the Seed and the Soil.

Most of the sermons I have heard preached on it have focussed on the seed and the soil, God's word and the recipients of that word; and on the contrasting outcomes. And indeed, this is what Jesus concentrated upon when he explained the parable to his disciples.

When I came to preach on it, I decided to look at the Sower.

At first glance he seems a pretty careless chap doesn't he? Seed was a precious commodity in those days, almost a currency. A good yield is critical to a good harvest; a good harvest critical to life. The key to this was good seed, carefully sown into well prepared and cultivated ground. And yet here's this guy chucking it all over the place!

Why? And who is this fellow?

Well, in the parable, the seed is the message about the kingdom. The Sower can be anyone who is spreading the word. But, at the time of the parable, the man doing the most spreading was Jesus. So, let's consider this an autobiographical parable, with Jesus in the lead role.

Was he being careless, irresponsible and wasting precious seed by preaching to all and sundry (even Samaritans and lepers)?

Or was he being lavishly and lovingly extravagant? Making sure that everyone had the opportunity to hear about and to receive God's grace.

I know what I think. How about you?

The other reason I love this parable is that I'm an adman and I learned my trade during the golden years of advertising in the 70s and 80s. Building big brands during the days of mass-audience TV and mass-market broadcast print media.

We didn't worry too much about Google analytics-style precision targeting then. We just ran interesting and entertaining ads conveying a strong brand message to a mass audience and waited for people to react. Of course, not everyone became a buyer, but the return on investment from those that did was huge. And even if people didn't buy the product, they still talked about the ad which helped fuel word of mouth.

There's a clear message here to the church today, and to anyone who wants to help get the word out:be extravagant; take a risk.

Let's not be too hung-up about getting God's word out to exactly the 'right' people, at just the 'right' time in precisely the 'right' way. Let's be like the Sower and just throw it out big time!

How can I help
spread the Word?

What is this story saying to me, here and now?

Heaven is...

HEAVEN IS LIKE...

Have you ever tried to explain to someone what Heaven is like? If so, you've probably discovered that it's not as easy as it might seem.

But, don't worry, you're in good company.

In this series of stories, Jesus had several goes at it.

STORY 1: JUNK MAIL

JUNK MAIL

Anusha Kapur closed the folder and placed it on the desk. With her chin resting upon steepled fingers she looked intently at the man sitting opposite her.

'How long have you worked for the Grantchester Gazette, Rob?'

'Just over five years.'

'And always in IT?'

'Yep.'

'Hmmm. Well, I've only been here as editor for three months, and so, clearly, I don't know our systems as well as you. But I've been a journalist for 12 years and what I can tell you is that this proposal to install a high-grade email filter is completely unacceptable.'

Rob bristled and leaned forward in his chair.

'Why on earth not, Anusha? I've studied our working practices and I can tell you that having this new filter will reduce the average inbox size by 60% and so massively increase productivity. Do you realise just how much time our journalists spend sifting through their emails? The return on investment will be huge.'

'No, no, it's not a matter of cost Rob. Look, the reason that journalists spend so much time ploughing through emails is that they're looking for stories. Good stories. The trouble is that they take some finding, because they are not always obvious. And a lot of them come from quite dubious sources, so an aggressive junk mail filter would have a heyday. I'm sure you are right that inbox sizes would drop by 60%, maybe even more. But I'm equally sure that we'd lose more than 60% of our stories.

'I'm sorry Rob, but our journalists are going to have to carry on doing what they've always done. Open their inboxes, work their way through all their emails, root out the good stories and only then hit the delete button on the remainder.'

Once Rob had left the office, Anusha picked up the folder and gently slid it into her waste bin.

The parable of the weeds

Matthew 13:24–30

24 Jesus told them another parable: 'The kingdom of heaven is like a man who sowed good seed in his field. 25 But while everyone was sleeping, his enemy came and sowed weeds among the wheat, and went away. 26 When the wheat sprouted and formed heads, then the weeds also appeared.

27 'The owner's servants came to him and said, "Sir, didn't you sow good seed in your field? Where then did the weeds come from?"

28 "'An enemy did this," he replied.

'The servants asked him, "Do you want us to go and pull them up?"

29 "'No," he answered, "because while you are pulling the weeds, you may uproot the wheat with them. 30 Let both grow together until the harvest. At that time I will tell the harvesters: First collect the weeds and tie them in bundles to be burned; then gather the wheat and bring it into my barn."'

> *But while everyone was sleeping, his enemy came and sowed weeds among the wheat, and went away*
>
> MATTHEW 13:25

So, what's this story saying to us, here and now?

In the story that Jesus told the weeds were sown by an enemy. A deliberate act of sabotage.

To be honest, I'm not sure I've completely captured that aspect of the parable in my rewiring. Although those of us who have suffered from spammers clogging up our inbox, or pop-up ads slowing down our web searches may well regard the perpetrators as an enemy!

However, the fact that it is subject to external attack shows just how good Heaven must be. And that, I think, is the point for us.

Heaven is worth getting really, really, excited about. But it is so good, that we must also be aware that the Devil is trying his wily best to stop us getting there.

We have been warned. Let's keep our eyes on the prize.

How might Satan
be obstructing me?

What is this story saying to me, here and now?

STORY 2: THE PENSION FUND

THE PENSION FUND

Polly was by no means rich. In fact, as a single parent (her husband having run off with another woman shortly after the birth of their son) she often found it hard to make ends meet.

When Jack was five he started school and Polly was able to resume her job as a primary school teacher. At the same school, which was convenient. The pay wasn't huge, but at least it paid the bills.

Then one day she received an unexpected windfall. A bequest from her Great Aunt.

What to do? Take Jack to Disneyland? Buy a new car?

Both were attractive options, but Polly took some time to think ahead and instead invested the money into a personal pension fund.

Then she got on with her life.

And whilst she did her job (rising to become head teacher of the school) the fund managers got on with theirs, and the fund grew.

Thirty years later she was ready to retire.

By which time Jack had been through university; pursued a lucrative career in the City; married and had two kids.

And Polly's personal pension had grown considerably, such that her retirement was better than her wildest hopes.

So much so that she was able to take a tax-free sum, buy a new car and take Jack, his wife and her grandchildren to Disneyland.

The parable of the growing seed

Mark 4:26-29

[26] *He also said, 'This is what the kingdom of God is like. A man scatters seed on the ground.* [27] *Night and day, whether he sleeps or gets up, the seed sprouts and grows, though he does not know how.* [28] *All by itself the soil produces grain - first the stalk, then the head, then the full kernel in the head.* [29] *As soon as the grain is ripe, he puts the sickle to it, because the harvest has come.'*

Night and day, whether he sleeps or gets up, the seed sprouts and grows

MARK 4:27

So, what's this story saying to us, here and now?

Jesus was keen to point out that God's kingdom is immeasurably better than anything we can possibly imagine (which is what makes it so difficult to describe); but also, that it has its roots, its origins, in the way we live our life.

In that sense, Heaven really is a place on earth.

Jesus used the analogy of someone planting seeds to grow a crop. I've rewired it as a pension fund growing from Polly's initial payment.

Neither Polly nor the seed-planter knew for certain what the return would be on their investment; neither quite understood how it all happened. It was beyond their control.

It was the result of an act of faith.

God's kingdom is also reached by an act of faith. Once we have committed ourselves to Jesus we can get on and live out our life of faith, secure in the knowledge that somehow, somewhere, completely beyond our control, God is preparing a future for us that is beyond our wildest dreams.

Now that sure sounds like Heaven to me.

What might my 'final
dividend' look like?

What is this story saying to me, here and now?

STORIES 3 & 4: LOOK UP AND LOOK IN

LOOK UP AND LOOK IN

If you want a picture of Heaven, think of it as a landmark building like the Millennium Stadium (since re-named as the Principality Stadium) in Cardiff. It started off as a single brick but grew into a structure that seats huge, vibrant, multinational crowds enjoying a spectacular, shared experience. Or the Shard, where the foundation stone supports a massive building that is home to many businesses, several luxury apartments, three restaurants and a five-star hotel. Or the modern hospice movement that started as one building in South East London and now exists worldwide, providing love and care for millions of patients and their families.

Think too of *Flower of Scotland* being sung at Murrayfield, which may start as a lone voice but grows and swells until it encompasses the whole stadium. Or a Mexican wave started by a small group at Anfield, but which eventually has 50,000 people participating. Or a cup of water poured into the Pacific, the molecules of which spread globally to the extent that some of them will be present in another cup of water taken from the Atlantic just months later.

The parables of the mustard seed and the yeast

Matthew 13:31–33

31 He told them another parable:'The kingdom of heaven is like a mustard seed, which a man took and planted in his field. 32 Though it is the smallest of all seeds, yet when it grows, it is the largest of garden plants and becomes a tree, so that the birds come and perch in its branches.'

33 He told them still another parable:'The kingdom of heaven is like yeast that a woman took and mixed into about sixty pounds of flour until it worked all through the dough.'

Mark 4:30–32

30 Again he said, 'What shall we say the kingdom of God is like, or what parable shall we use to describe it? 31 It is like a mustard seed, which is the smallest of all seeds on earth. 32 Yet when planted, it grows and becomes the largest of all garden plants, with such big branches that the birds can perch in its shade.'

Luke 13:18–21

18 Then Jesus asked, 'What is the kingdom of God like? What shall I compare it to? 19 It is like a mustard seed, which a man took and planted in his garden. It grew and became a tree, and the birds perched in its branches.'

20 Again he asked, 'What shall I compare the kingdom of God to? 21 It is like yeast that a woman took and mixed into about thirty kilograms of flour until it worked all through the dough.'

> *The kingdom of heaven is like a mustard seed, which a man took and planted in his field*
> MARK 4:27

So, what's this story saying to us, here and now?

Jesus is seeking to give some tangibility to an otherwise fairly abstract concept.

A mustard seed and yeast are living organisms.

I've tried to extend that into a greater sense of physicality in my rewiring. And add a sense of community and participation.

Many people will see Heaven as an ethereal, intangible place. Angels, harps and clouds.

No, says Jesus. It's as real, more real, than all the places you have ever visited or experiences you have ever shared and enjoyed on earth.

As real as the Millennium Stadium and the Shard; Murrayfield and the Pacific Ocean.

Heaven is all these and more.

But, getting back to the mustard seed and yeast, the other point about living organisms is that they grow and expand.

In that respect, Heaven has no maximum capacity. So, let's make sure it includes you and me.

Especially as Jesus has already paid our price of admission.

Do I have my
ticket to Heaven?

What is this story saying to me, here and now?

STORIES 5 & 6: THE PENNY AND THE CARP

THE PENNY AND THE CARP

The queen's head swam into view and grew larger as the glass hovered over it. A pair of eyes blinked and then focussed on the tiny KN etched onto the truncated neck. It was indeed a 1919 penny struck at Kings Norton and in near mint condition.

Dennis Rowland's life had taken a distinct down-turn in recent years. First his electrical wholesale business had failed. Shortly after, his wife walked off with one of his best friends. And hard on the heels of that he suffered a pulmonary embolism that left him hospitalised with a collapsed lung. To cap it all, whilst he was recuperating the bank foreclosed on his mortgage.

His mum had come to the rescue. Widowed a few years earlier, she had an annexe in her house going spare and she would relish her son's company. They would be close to each other without being on top of each other. It was a Godsend. And it was followed by a few other bright spots as his finances recovered:the liquidation of his business and the sale of his house raising some cash. And he found some part-time work repping for an electrical manufacturer. Things were looking up again.

Dennis and his mum found they enjoyed each other's company and, on his birthday, she retrieved his boyhood coin collection from the attic and presented it to him. Dennis was delighted. The highlight of his collection were the old pennies that he had started to collect after they had been phased out in 1971.

He now had the money to fill in some of the missing years and upgrade the condition of others. So, he was delighted at finding a 1919KN in such good condition.

A few days later, a sales trip took him to Worksop. Whilst there he dropped into an antique shop.

He mentioned his particular interest in coins and the owner asked if he would like to see a large collection that had just arrived. It was part of the estate of a local person. Its highlight was a magnificent collection of gold sovereigns, so the £20,000 price tag was understandable. And totally out of Dennis' league. But as a keen numismatist he wanted to see it just out of interest. As he looked through it, his eyes nearly popped out of his head. There was a collection of pennies including one from 1933. 1933! The rarest penny of them all. None had been officially minted, but over the years six had turned up:probably having found their way out in the trouser pockets of workers at the mint.

In numismatic circles it was priceless.

Dennis asked if he could buy just the pennies but was told that the executors felt the owner would not have wanted to see the collection broken up.

Dennis returned home and did his sums. If he took all his savings, sold his car and cashed in an endowment policy he could raise £20,000 and the collection, including the 1933 penny, would be his.

So, he did. And it was.

Jesus pauses, takes a swig of Lucozade and launches into his follow-up story:

The waters rippled. The line trembled, tightened. The rod struck.

Tamsin Chadwick was a high-flying PR executive. She had a silver tongue and a golden touch. Aged 57, she now owned her own consultancy with a client list full of A-listers from the film and music industry. Unmarried, with a penthouse apartment in Kensington, her job was her life.

Except it wasn't her total life. Because she had a hobby that was very dear to her. She was an angler. More specifically, a carp angler. Even more specifically a specimen carp angler. She pursued specimen carp with as much commitment and skill as she would pursue her next rock star client.

But whereas her aim with clients was to hang onto them for as long as possible, when it came to carp she operated a strict catch, snap and release policy. The walls of her room were adorned by photos of shiny live fish rather than stuffed dead ones.

Her hobby took her to all the top carp-fishing locations around the UK and Europe, the best of which were as expensive as skiing in Méribel.

This weekend she had booked a cottage set beside a lake in the heart of middle England. A tranquil, bucolic spot set in a sprawling country estate.

It was there that she hooked the biggest carp she had ever seen in her life. But not only had she hooked the carp, but the carp, lake and its setting had hooked her.

On the spot she decided upon a complete life change. She wanted to be here. To fish this lake (which she suspected was bulging with prize carp), to enjoy this lovely spot, to live a new lifestyle. But to do this she would have to buy not just the lake, but the 2,000 acres and country mansion that went with it. Ever the decisive business person, she returned to London, sold her business, sold her apartment, sold her Bentley and Ferrari.

And the deal was done.

The parables of the hidden treasure and the pearl

Matthew 13:44–46

[44] *'The kingdom of heaven is like treasure hidden in a field. When a man found it, he hid it again, and then in his joy went and sold all he had and bought that field.*

[45] *'Again, the kingdom of heaven is like a merchant looking for fine pearls.* [46] *When he found one of great value, he went away and sold everything he had and bought it.'*

> *The kingdom of heaven is like treasure hidden in a field*
>
> MATTHEW 13:44

So, what's this story saying to us, here and now?

What is your most precious possession?

Let's put it another way, if your house were on fire, what would be the first thing you would rescue?

(And I'm talking about material objects here, not people – so, the answer is not your children/spouse/parents/grandparents/pet dog etc. It's not that they are not precious to you; simply that they are not the answer I want to the question I am posing!)

A lot of people have said that the first thing they would seek to rescue would be their family photos. But as more and more of those become digital, scanned and otherwise backed up on iCloud and OneDrive, so it forces us to confront the question again.

I'll now widen it:what is your most precious or *most desired* possession? And what would you pay to replace it or gain it?

Ah, now it gets tricky doesn't it. We start to feel grubbily materialistic. (My thoughts are already spinning towards something red, with four wheels and a prancing horse logo.)

But, hang on a moment, Jesus talked about treasure and pearls. They are pretty materialistic!

So, I'll ask again.

What is your most precious or most desired possession? And what would you pay to replace it or gain it?

Please try and give an answer. I'll wait a while and let you think.

There you go, not so difficult was it! Or maybe it was. And that doesn't matter. It's not the point.

Clearly, I don't know the answer. But what I can tell you is that, whatever it is, Heaven is worth far, far more.

Everything we have, in fact.

That's what these two stories are saying to us, here and now.

I'll leave you alone again to think of the implications.

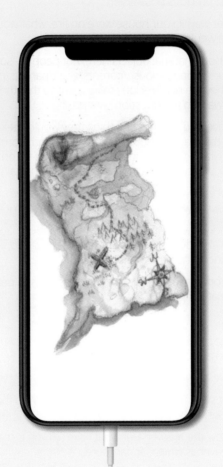

Where does Heaven
rank on my wish list?

What is this story saying to me, here and now?

STORY 7: THE JOB APPLICATIONS

THE JOB APPLICATIONS

'Well done people, let's break for coffee.'

Two piles of paper sat on the desk, one considerably higher than the other.

Director of Human Resources, Megan Williams, addressed her team:

'So, we've reduced the applications from 115 to 17; and we've done that by being pretty ruthless in our assessment of their qualifications, experience and character.

'But then this is a critical position we are trying to fill. The Head of Public Relations is the public face of the company. He or she will have no room for error due to the awful mistakes that were made over our recent product recall. Whoever we appoint must hit the ground running. We cannot afford to get this appointment wrong.

'Now comes the even tougher part of the exercise. These 17 applications need to be scrutinised again.'

The team groaned inwardly but brightened at their Director's next remark.

'But, don't worry,' she said, 'I'll do it, here and now.'

The team then looked on amazed as she quickly sifted through the papers and sorted six into a pile on the right of the desk and 11 to the left. She then picked up these 11 and gave them to the team leader. 'Here you go,' she said, 'you can put these with the other rejects, and we'll ask these six in for interviews.'

She was heading back to her office when something in the atmosphere stopped her. She turned around and faced the puzzled faces.

'Ah, I guess you're wondering how I decided so quickly. It's quite simple actually. We asked each applicant to name two CEOs who they really admired. Three of those 11 gave just one name:they over-simplified the question; the other eight gave more than two names:they over-complicated it. Either way, they all ignored a clear brief and that's an unacceptable trait in a senior PR person.'

The parable of the net

Matthew 13:47–50

[47] 'Once again, the kingdom of heaven is like a net that was let down into the lake and caught all kinds of fish. [48] When it was full, the fishermen pulled it up on the shore. Then they sat down and collected the good fish in baskets, but threw the bad away. [49] This is how it will be at the end of the age. The angels will come and separate the wicked from the righteous [50] and throw them into the blazing furnace, where there will be weeping and gnashing of teeth.'

Once again, the kingdom of heaven is like a net that was let down into the lake and caught all kinds of fish

MATTHEW 13:47

So, what's this story saying to us, here and now?

The first of these stories, the Weeds, showed us how the enemy, Satan to give him a name, is desperately trying to send his acolytes to infiltrate Heaven, to rob us of our inheritance.

In the 1980s, Robert Maxwell sought to do exactly that:to send in his accountants to steal the pension funds of his own employees.

For those of us in work and paying into a pension at the time, it caused us to look very carefully at the security of our own positions.

Myself included.

I switched my company pension into a personal pension.

No way was I going to have my pension fund raided and my family's future stolen.

So, this story resonates very strongly with me.

It reassures us once again, that Satan won't succeed in his attempts to infiltrate heaven.

No way are his followers going to make it in!

I'm extremely, supremely, glad that Megan Williams, the fishermen and the angels are there protecting my and my family's spiritual, eternal future.

I sleep sounder every night as a result.

ZZZZZZZZZZ

How secure am I
in my faith?
(1 Peter 5:8)

What is this story saying to me, here and now?

STORY 8: THE WINE MERCHANT

THE WINE MERCHANT

'I am sorry monsieur, but we do not sell American wines.'

The customer looked puzzled. 'But we're having stew tonight and I want to serve a big red with it. Preferably a Napa Cabernet Sauvignon.'

Claude gave a Gallic shrug of the shoulders.

'Ok, well what do you have in the way of Shiraz?'

'I am sorry sir, but we do not sell Australian wines either. Or South African, before you ask.'

Now the customer looked annoyed. 'Ok, I'll just have to go to the supermarket.'

'Yes sir, I think you should.'

Claude Mignolet owns a wine shop in Norwich, or as he would put it, *the* wine shop in Norwich. Ever since it opened, it has been stocked almost exclusively with French wines (although a thorough search of the premises may occasionally reveal a fine Barolo, Amarone or Rioja).

Claude, like his father before him, has been a staunch believer that true wine comes only from the 'Old World'.

His nephew, Pierre, has a job that requires him to travel extensively around the world. The job also comes with a generous expense account, giving him the opportunity to try fine wines from all parts. He would often try to persuade Claude to stock at least a Napa Cabernet or a Marlborough Sauvignon Blanc. But Claude was having none of it.

Imagine then Pierre's shock, and delight, when he calls into the shop one day and finds it transformed.

As he enters the door he is presented with, to his left, a section signed as 'Old World'. The venerable French, Italian and Spanish classics take pride of place here, and Pierre even spots a German Riesling.

To his right he encounters 'New World'. Browsing the shelves here he finds top vintages from the USA, Chile, Argentina, Australia, New Zealand and a host of other countries. There is even an English sparkling white.

'Uncle Claude, I'm amazed. What's happened?'

'My boy, I admit that I am a traditionalist, but I am not as stuck in my ways as you may think. I have been carefully investigating these new wines for several years now and quietly building my cellars, so that I can offer the very best of the new alongside the very best of the old.'

Pierre continues to wander, amazed, around the shop. 'Uncle, this is absolutely superb. I feel like I have died and gone to Heaven.'

The parable of the owner of the house

Matthew 13:51–52

51 'Have you understood all these things?' Jesus asked. 'Yes,' they replied. 52 He said to them, 'Therefore every teacher of the law who has become a disciple in the kingdom of heaven is like the owner of a house who brings out of his storeroom new treasures as well as old.'

"

Have you understood all these things?' Jesus asked

MATTHEW 13:51

So, what's this story saying to us, here and now?

Wine occupied quite a prominent place in Jesus' ministry and teaching, so I was keen to feature it in one of my rewired parables.

This one provided the perfect opportunity!

It's the eighth and last story in the 'Heaven is like' series and, as verse 51 indicates, brings them all together.

What I particularly like about this story is the way that old and new exist harmoniously, side by side. The new has not come to replace the old; and the old does not try to invalidate the new. A perfect change management scenario.

And what Jesus seems to be saying here is that in Heaven everything will be brought together and reconciled. Past, present and future:all believers across all countries, civilisations and cultures. All relationships across family and friends, past, present and future. A vast storeroom of treasures old and treasures new; Old World wines and New World wines.

A new Heaven and a new Earth echoing Isaiah 65:17 and pointing towards Revelation 21:1.

What a powerful, exciting vision!

What's my vision of
Heaven?

What is this story saying to me, here and now?

...Heaven is

IT SURE FEELS LIKE HEAVEN TO ME!

If anyone is qualified to talk about Heaven, it's Jesus!

But I sense that even he was struggling to find the words, the best way to describe it.

(No surprise there really. Heaven is not of this world.)

But, individually, these eight stories each give us some tantalising glimpses:

The parable of the *weeds* shows that it's worth getting excited about. Why else would the enemy, the devil, be trying to infiltrate it, to pollute it, to prevent us from attaining it.

The *growing seed* shows us how God is preparing an eternal future for us that is beyond our wildest dreams.

I really like the imagery of the *mustard seed* and the *yeast*. They present Heaven as a living organism, growing and expanding; huge and filling the world with its goodness.

The *hidden treasure* and the *pearl* re-affirm how precious Heaven is. Priceless in fact. Something worth giving everything else up for.

And the *net* reassures us that the enemy will not penetrate Heaven. This is a place exclusively reserved for God and his friends. It's safe and it's secure.

Taken together, collectively, these first seven stories start to build up a sense of the true Heaven; in our hearts and souls rather than our minds.

And the eighth story, the *owner of the house*, confirms and affirms it all. How great it is to know that come the day, we shall see a new Heaven and a new Earth as the two come together.

And how great it is to know also that our faith in Jesus means that we are assured of a place there.

Which is why Jesus is so keen to give us a sense of what it will be like.

A final thought.

Have you ever had a wonderful feeling of peace, contentment and fulfilment come over you? Maybe whilst sharing time with someone very close and dear to you; maybe prompted by a stunning sight of nature, a piece of music or art; holding a newborn baby in your arms. Or maybe during a time of quiet, prayerful, reflection.

It may be that, for those few moments, we experience a 'taster' of Heaven.

And wow, isn't it *good*!

THE TALE OF THE TWO DRIVERS

The disciples asked Jesus to increase their faith. His response was that faith is absolute; either you have it, or you don't. It cannot be increased or decreased. He also said to keep in mind who and what you are having faith in and why. Oh, and he told them this story:

It was a cold night on Park Lane. The wind howled down the road from Marble Arch to Hyde Park Corner like a Siberian express train.

A line of stationary executive cars snaked along the kerbside outside the Dorchester Hotel's ballroom entrance. Each was occupied by a single figure, many wearing the peaked cap that still seems to be the obligatory mark of office for a professional chauffeur.

It had just turned midnight, but it would be another hour before their charges came boiling out of the hotel looking for a fast ride home.

One of the drivers stepped out of his car and tucking his head against the wind walked down the line to a black Mercedes S-Class and knocked on the passenger door. Seeing him, the driver disabled the central locking and the man climbed in.

'Wotcha Dwyane,' said the driver.

'Hiya Denny. Heck of a night, I reckon it will be sleeting within the hour.'

'You could well be right there,' Denny replied. He pulled out a Thermos flask. 'Fancy a cuppa?'

Dwyane gratefully accepted the steaming cup. 'How's it going with you and your guvnor? He's a cold fish isn't he. I've never seen him give you a word of thanks. Does he talk much in the car?'

'Not to me, no, but that's just his way. Mostly he's on the phone.'

'Well my bloke is always chatting to me and asking about the wife and kids and what we're all up to. Got a good stock of jokes as well.'

Denny shrugged. 'I guess my guy is just too focussed on his job. As well as driving him, I run his wife around, pick the kids up from school, wash their cars, even do shopping for them occasionally.'

'Cor, what a liberty!'

'Well, it takes all types. And the way I see it, I'm there to make his life easier – that's my job. And as the saying goes, if a job's worth doing it's worth doing well. Plus, if I look after his needs, I like to believe he'll look after mine. Incidentally, Dwyane, what's your rate of pay?'

'Fifteen pounds an hour. What's yours?'

'Thirty...'

The parable of the master and his servant

Luke 17:5–10

⁵ *The apostles said to the Lord, 'Increase our faith!'*

⁶ *He replied, 'If you have faith as small as a mustard seed, you can say to this mulberry tree, "Be uprooted and planted in the sea," and it will obey you.*

⁷ *'Suppose one of you has a servant ploughing or looking after the sheep. Will he say to the servant when he comes in from the field, "Come along now and sit down to eat"? ⁸ Won't he rather say, "Prepare my supper, get yourself ready and wait on me while I eat and drink; after that you may eat and drink"? ⁹ Will he thank the servant because he did what he was told to do? ¹⁰ So you also, when you have done everything you were told to do, should say, "We are unworthy servants; we have only done our duty."'*

The apostles said to the Lord, 'Increase our faith!'
LUKE 17:5

So, what's this story saying to us, here and now?

Ours is a very egalitarian culture, a democracy in which we all have equal stakes. This is fuelled by the media who allow us to get up close and personal with famous people. It allows us to understand them better as people. And, like all people, they have their strengths and shortcomings.

In some ways, this exposure is a good thing. It instils greater accountability within those in a position of authority and it can also make them appear somewhat more approachable.

But, it does have some downsides. (The obvious one being invasion of privacy, but that is not the substance of this parable.)

It can generate an over-familiarity between the public and the authorities, which can then breed a general lack of respect for institutions and individuals. We see this in pupil attitudes to teachers; public attitudes to police officers and the way soccer players abuse the referee.

And, unwittingly, we can get a bit full of ourselves; develop an overblown sense of our own importance. The 'me culture'.

Our mindset is that all authorities:royalty, government, local authorities, employers, banks, shops are there to serve us, not vice-versa.

Consumerism rules, ok!

Maybe that is not entirely a bad thing (a would-be dictator would hate it for instance) providing it is kept in balance.

But we do have to be extremely careful that we don't let it spill over into our relationship with God. That's what this parable addresses.

God loves us, encourages us to talk with him and even sent his son to live among us as one of us. He wants an intimate relationship with us.

But he is also our Lord, our master and our creator. The ultimate authority on earth and across time and space.

We must guard against intimacy becoming over-familiarity.

Our prayer, our praise and our worship, even at its most

spontaneous and informal, must always be underpinned by a sense of awe and respect.

And, critically, we must always be very clear on who is serving who.

Our task is to serve God's agenda, not vice-versa.

Jesus tells this parable to the apostles in response to their request to him that he increase their faith. In essence, he is telling them not to get carried away and be seduced by a sense of their own position and importance. They are there to serve God and God has given them enough faith for all that he wants them to achieve.

And so it is with us. It is when we feel that we have really achieved great things for God that we can be at our most vulnerable.

It can breed within us too great a sense of our own 'holiness'.

Or it can lead to a conditional, even contractual relationship:'I've done great things for you God, now what are you going to do for me?'

My suspicion is that at some time or other this happens to most of us:it certainly does to me. It has even happened in the course of writing this book.

So, if ever you catch yourself being a bit over-familiar with God, taking liberties from the relationship, read this parable.

And, whilst the wages of sin are not particularly attractive, the wages of obedient duty are very good indeed.

So, take encouragement from Denny; faithful service that goes above and beyond the call of duty will bring its own rewards.

How awesome
is my God!

What is this story saying to me, here and now?

THE CASE OF THE VINDICTIVE LANDLORD

Jesus was asked, by Peter, whether there was a limit on how many times we should forgive somebody. Anyone who has been persistently wronged by someone may feel this is a reasonable question. But Jesus told this story as a seemingly quite unreasonable response:

Scene 1:The phone call
'Oh no, you cannot be serious. There is no way you can cancel a tenancy agreement because the tenant has missed just one month's payment. Look, he's a really good friend of mine:it's only £500, I'll make the payment for him.'

'Well, I am serious. I can cancel it and I shall,' the landlord replied. 'I have a buyer who for some reason that I don't care about wants to pay stupid money for this house and I can make a good turn on it. Fortunately for me, my tenant has defaulted so he can go swing and I can make a real killing. It's really touching that you want to make the payment but it's too late. Maybe you can buy him a caravan – and move in with him as you're such good friends.'

A mocking laugh ended the conversation and the phone line went dead as he hung up.

Scene 2:The inquest
Across town a lawyer steeled himself for a very tricky meeting with his boss Paul Croucher, the owner of Croucher Estates, a multi-millionaire who had built a business from a one room-let house to a property empire that encompassed residential, commercial and retail property development and leasing.

It would be a tricky meeting because a major error had come to light in the finance department.

As they had prepared to transfer the deeds on a large residential property, an assistant in the legal department had noticed that the mortgagee had been paying £660 per month rather than the £6,600 as stipulated in the contract. Someone had missed a zero! The upshot was that, over a 25-year mortgage term, the mortgagee had underpaid by nearly £1.8 million.

'Yes Paul, it's a major human error that occurred 25 years ago, and yes it should have been picked up at some point, so it's also a major systems error. We can't do anything now about the human error, but we can and already have amended the system to make sure such a thing can't happen again.

'Meantime, we have a cast-iron legal case for demanding that the underpayment be made before we transfer the deeds. This guy signed the original contract and there is no way he cannot have known he was underpaying. We are even within our rights to foreclose on him if we want. I say we get him in and have it out.'

Scene 3:The meeting
So, later that day Paul, the lawyer and Brian Langford, the mortgagee, sat around a polished mahogany meeting table. The atmosphere was tense, adversarial. No coffee and biscuits were being served. The lawyer laid out the case, which culminated in a demand for an immediate payment of £1,782,000. To his surprise, Langford did not contest it. Instead he burst into tears.

There followed an embarrassing few moments and then Langford pulled himself together. 'Look, I'm really sorry, but I'm a builder, not an accountant. I contract out all my financial administration and they never said anything to me. I've spent 25 years building this business. I haven't the cash to make that size of payment; and I can't afford to lose that building. Either way, I would be bankrupted.'

He appealed directly to Paul Croucher:'Have you never made a mistake that you regretted?'

Paul signalled to the lawyer and the two men left the room.

In his office he sighed. 'Jack, I don't believe for a moment that he didn't know what was going on, and I can't stand the crocodile tears. But, I do believe him when he says this would bankrupt him and I don't feel comfortable forcing anyone out of business. Plus, our system should really have picked it up. Tell him we're going to write off the underpayment.'

The lawyer went back into the meeting room and gave the news to Langford, who, amazed at his good fortune, left the building with a spring in his step and made a short journey across town to the local law courts.

Scene 4:The showdown
Here a judge was due to pass judgment on the plea for unfair eviction that his tenant had brought against him. Langford received his second piece of unexpectedly good news that day as the judge ruled that, whilst unfair and verging on the immoral, the eviction was not in fact illegal and must stand.

As the tenant sat stunned, his friend arrived in the courtroom to comfort him.

It had taken Paul Croucher slightly longer to get across town, but he was still in time to see exactly who it was that was evicting his good friend. When Langford saw him, he did not even have the grace to look abashed; instead he gave a sardonic smile.

Paul's eyes bored deeply back into him as he reached into his pocket and pulled out his mobile phone. Still holding his glare, he hit a speed dial:'Jack, about that huge underpayment we just decided to write off. A change of plan. Call in the debt. If the guy can't pay, we'll take all his business assets instead.'

The parable of the unmerciful servant

Matthew 18:21–35

21 Then Peter came to Jesus and asked, 'Lord, how many times shall I forgive my brother or sister who sins against me? Up to seven times?'

22 Jesus answered, 'I tell you, not seven times, but seventy-seven times.

23 'Therefore, the kingdom of heaven is like a king who wanted to settle accounts with his servants. 24 As he began the settlement, a man who owed him ten thousand bags of gold was brought to him. 25 Since he was not able to pay, the master ordered that he and his wife and his children and all that he had be sold to repay the debt.

26 'At this the servant fell on his knees before him. "Be patient with me," he begged, "and I will pay back everything." 27 The servant's master took pity on him, cancelled the debt and let him go.

28 'But when that servant went out, he found one of his fellow servants who owed him a hundred silver coins. He grabbed him and began to choke him. "Pay back what you owe me!" he demanded.

29 'His fellow servant fell to his knees and begged him, "Be patient with me, and I will pay it back."

30 'But he refused. Instead, he went off and had the man thrown into prison until he could pay the debt. 31 When the other servants saw what had happened, they were outraged and went and told their master everything that had happened.

32 'Then the master called the servant in. "You wicked servant," he said, "I cancelled all that debt of yours because you begged me to. 33 Shouldn't you have had mercy on your fellow servant just as I had on you?" 34 In anger his master handed him over to the jailers to be tortured, until he should pay back all he owed.

35 'This is how my heavenly Father will treat each of you unless you forgive your brother or sister from your heart.'

Lord, how many times shall I forgive my brother or sister who sins against me?
MATTHEW 18:21

So, what's this story saying to us, here and now?

It's a tough question to ask ourselves, isn't it:'Have I ever wronged anyone?'

It's even tougher to digest the answer!

The fact is that most of us have wronged someone in our lives, even if by accident and unintentionally.

So, there is going to be someone whose forgiveness we need, for whatever reason.

The corollary of that is that there will be at least one person who needs our forgiveness, for whatever reason.

And all of us need, and have received, God's forgiveness of course.

I'm not going to trivialise this topic by saying something like:'so we should all be forgiving'.

The truth is that forgiving someone can be extremely difficult when that person has done you or, worse, someone close to you, some major wrong – harm even. I've experienced that and I'm sure that many of you reading this will have too.

But what this parable urges us to do is to always consider how we should bestow forgiveness in the context of the forgiveness we have received for ourselves:from others and from God. And, even if we find it beyond our capability to forgive now, to continue to reflect and pray on it.

Because there is one further aspect we must take into account.

Unforgiveness is frequently accompanied by its twin sibling, bitterness. But, the object of that bitterness, the wrongdoer, is unaffected by it. The only person hurt by such bitterness is the person who holds it. In extreme cases, the victim of a wrongdoing can find themselves being held prisoner by the bitterness they hold against the perpetrator.

I have heard more than one person talk of the sense of personal release, inner peace and freedom they have experienced when, sometimes years after the incident, they have finally been able to forgive and let go.

No wonder Jesus was so insistent on the need for us to exercise forgiveness.

Maybe I can't forget,
but can I forgive?

What is this story saying to me, here and now?

THE COMPASSIONATE MILLWALL FAN

The teachers of the law were a pernickety bunch and constantly looking for a way of tripping Jesus up. They never succeeded, but that didn't stop them trying!

Here an 'expert in the law' hoped to entangle Jesus in a definition debate:"When you say, 'love your neighbour', who exactly is my neighbour?"

As always, Jesus came up with a stunning response:

My friend, Jermaine, a sports teacher, went on a day-trip with some of his mates to Marseille to watch England play Russia in Euro 2016. Before he even arrived at the ground the group he was in was caught up in fights and riots between rival supporters. It was nothing to do with him, of course, it was just his misfortune to be in the wrong place at the wrong time. He became separated from the rest of his group and was badly beaten up. He was also robbed of his wallet, match tickets and, crucially, his passport. He was hurt, his clothes were ripped, he was bloodied, and he needed help.

The police were worse than useless and indeed he only narrowly avoided being arrested. He remembers asking various people for help. A young couple, some other businessmen, some girls, even someone who appeared to be a priest. No-one was prepared to help. Maybe because they thought he was a dangerous hooligan. Maybe because they just didn't want to get involved. Maybe because they were in too much of a hurry to get to the game (by now it was getting towards kick-off). Whatever, they walked on by and Jermaine was becoming desperate.

He became even more alarmed when a 17-stone, bare-torsoed, garishly-tattooed Millwall supporter arrived on the scene. Fearing another kicking, he tried to get away but was grabbed by the giant. To Jermaine's utter surprise, the guy sat him down and asked how he was. He gave him a drink, (beer not water but Jermaine wasn't complaining!) He asked where he was staying and on finding that Jermaine had no hotel, money or passport he hailed a taxi and took him to a nearby hotel. He then proceeded to book him in, leaving his own credit card as security, and then jumped back in the taxi to get to the game with a promise to return afterwards. Which he did.

Now, the question is:who was neighbour to my friend?

The legal eagle thought long and hard and then hesitantly replied:'The Millwall fan, because he had compassion.'

'Spot on, take a lead from him!'

The parable of the good Samaritan

Luke 10:25–37

²⁵ On one occasion an expert in the law stood up to test Jesus. 'Teacher,' he asked, 'what must I do to inherit eternal life?'

²⁶ 'What is written in the Law?' he replied. 'How do you read it?'

²⁷ He answered, 'Love the Lord your God with all your heart and with all your soul and with all your strength and with all your mind' and, 'Love your neighbour as yourself.'

²⁸ 'You have answered correctly,' Jesus replied. 'Do this and you will live.'

²⁹ But he wanted to justify himself, so he asked Jesus, 'And who is my neighbour?'

³⁰ In reply Jesus said: 'A man was going down from Jerusalem to Jericho, when he was attacked by robbers. They stripped him of his clothes, beat him and went away, leaving him half-dead. ³¹ A priest happened to be going down the same road, and when he saw the man, he passed by on the other side. ³² So too, a Levite, when he came to the place and saw him, passed by on the other side. ³³ But a Samaritan, as he travelled, came where the man was; and when he saw him, he took pity on him. ³⁴ He went to him and bandaged his wounds, pouring on oil and wine. Then he put the man on his own donkey, brought him to an inn and took care of him. ³⁵ The next day he took out two denarii and gave them to the innkeeper. "Look after him," he said, "and when I return, I will reimburse you for any extra expense you may have."

³⁶ 'Which of these three do you think was a neighbour to the man who fell into the hands of robbers?'

³⁷ The expert in the law replied, 'The one who had mercy on him.'

Jesus told him, 'Go and do likewise.'

> Which of these three do you think was a neighbour to the man who fell into the hands of robbers?
> LUKE 10:36

So, what's this story saying to us, here and now?

Jesus took the cosy concept of neighbourliness:people we know, people we like, people nearby, people like us; and blew it apart.

Neighbourliness he said, is not about physical proximity; it's an attitude of mind, a relationship with humanity as a whole.

The Jews hated Samaritans with a passion.

Jesus turned that prejudice against them.

I said that Jesus made a stunning response and the law expert would indeed have been almost literally stunned. First by the story, then by the logic that forced him to admit that a Samaritan had been a good neighbour.

We live in a world of 24-hour rolling news and global connectivity.

Never have we known our 'neighbours' better.

Do we allow that knowledge to confront our prejudices or just to confirm them?

It's an important question, because as Jesus points out in response to the law expert's first question, loving our neighbour is one of the keys to eternal life. And things don't get much more important than that!

Historical footnote
It's possible to interpret the concept of a 'neighbour' in two ways. In a metaphorical sense:any human being in need. And in a geographical sense:those physically closest to you.

In my hotwiring above, I've tried to link the two in a way that speaks to us today, here and now.

But, when Jesus first told the story it would have been radical teaching, in both senses of neighbourliness.

First, in Jewish culture, to suffer any kind of misfortune was regarded as a sign that you had sinned and incurred God's displeasure. The fault was yours and the solution was to mend your ways. This story blows that apart. When he said 'Go and do likewise' Jesus was telling his audience, and us, that we need to look beyond any 'labelling' of such people; instead to see them as God's creation that he loves and cares about.

Second, the closest neighbours to the Jews were the Samaritans, the inhabitants of Samaria. In times gone by, this had been the Northern Kingdom of Israel, with Judah forming the Southern Kingdom. For various reasons, a deep rift had developed between the two.

In Jesus' story a Samaritan shows love and compassion for a Jew. When he said 'Go and do likewise' Jesus was telling his audience to reconcile themselves with their closest neighbours, their ancestral brothers and sisters. To heal the family rift. Go, in love for them, to make things right with them.

And where was the first recorded Christian church to be established outside Jerusalem?

Yep, in Samaria (see Acts 8).

As Peter and John hastened there to confirm the new Samaritan Christians with the Holy Spirit, maybe Jesus' parable was still ringing in their ears!

So, a final thought:are you estranged with anyone that Jesus may want you to make things right with?

REFLECTION AND PRAYER

Is God calling me to be a neighbour to somebody? Anybody?

(Maybe even to somebody I don't actually like very much?)

What is this story saying to me, here and now?

THE PANICKING COLLEAGUE

The disciples asked Jesus to teach them how to pray. In response, he taught them what we now know as 'The Lord's Prayer'.

He also told them a story:

An alarm shrilled on the cabin speakers as the plane suddenly dropped like a stone.

It was pitch black, the cabin lights had failed.

The plane was de-pressurising.

He reached out frantically to grab an oxygen mask but couldn't locate one.

The alarm continued to shriek.

Then his hand brushed the clock radio.

And fastened upon the phone.

Cal fought his way up and through the dark blanket of tiredness and disorientation.

The alarm lit up:2.03 am.

As the phone rang again he cursed inwardly and tried to clear his head.

As he did so he realised he wasn't still on the plane.

His departure from Los Angeles had been delayed by a vicious summer storm.

Four hours in the plane on the tarmac followed by a 14-hour flight.

He had finally got home just before 1am and, jet-lagged, gone straight to bed.

He pressed the answer button, yawning.

'Cal, Cal, I'm really sorry but I need you to email me the Global Inc sales pitch.'

It was his friend, Tom, a colleague from the office.

'Tom, it's 2am, my wife and kids are – make that were – asleep and I've had just one hour's sleep myself. What's the panic? The meeting isn't until Wednesday.'

'No, no! I've just heard that the client is arriving tomorrow and wants the meeting then. I don't have a copy of the presentation on my system.'

'Yeah, well it will still keep until morning. Please don't ring back, you'll wake my wife and kids again.'

And with that, Cal pressed the hang up button.

But the hour's sleep was enough to now keep him awake

He cursed Tom.

'You may be my close buddy,' he muttered, 'but that was way out of order.'

But, as he lay there, other thoughts started running through his head

Poor guy must be really stressed...

He probably wants to get himself fully rehearsed...

It took a lot of guts to make that call...

And with that he slid quietly out of bed, padded downstairs to his computer and emailed the document.

Before he went back upstairs he sent a text to Tom:It's in your inbox. I'd have called you to say it's on the way, but didn't want to wake your wife and kids...

The parable of the friend in need

Luke 11:1–13

1 One day Jesus was praying in a certain place. When he finished, one of his disciples said to him, 'Lord, teach us to pray, just as John taught his disciples.'

2 He said to them, 'When you pray, say:

"'Father,
hallowed be your name,
your kingdom come.
3 Give us each day our daily bread.
4 Forgive us our sins,
for we also forgive everyone who sins against us.
And lead us not into temptation."'

5 Then Jesus said to them, 'Suppose you have a friend, and you go to him at midnight and say, "Friend, lend me three loaves of bread; 6 a friend of mine on a journey has come to me, and I have no food to offer him." 7 And suppose the one inside answers, "Don't bother me. The door is already locked, and my children and I are in bed. I can't get up and give you anything." 8 I tell you, even though he will not get up and give you the bread because of friendship, yet because of your shameless audacity he will surely get up and give you as much as you need.

9 'So I say to you: ask and it will be given to you; seek and you will find; knock and the door will be opened to you. 10 For everyone who asks receives; the one who seeks finds; and to the one who knocks, the door will be opened.

11 'Which of you fathers, if your son asks for a fish, will give him a snake instead? 12 Or if he asks for an egg, will give him a scorpion? 13 If you then, though you are evil, know how to give good gifts to your children, how much more will your Father in heaven give the Holy Spirit to those who ask him!'

Lord, teach us to pray
LUKE 11:1

So, what's this story saying to us, here and now?

'When you haven't a prayer, pray.'

It's amazing how even people who eschew God will instinctively endorse prayer when seeking to comfort others:

'I'll say a prayer for you'; 'You're in our thoughts & prayers'; 'Please God, things will get better.'

We see it too when times of national and international crisis result in a spike in church attendances:Cuban missiles; the death of Princess Diana; 9/11; 7/7. It's almost like an internal default switch is thrown within the national psyche.

'When you haven't a prayer, pray.'

I've long thought that hotwiring that line could lead to a powerful 'call to prayer' advertising campaign. It would start where people are at, address a need; and offer a clear benefit.

When you haven't a prayer, pray – there are worse ways to find a way to God.

Of course, us hardened Christian prayer warriors may turn up our noses and say something like:'prayer should be the first thing you use, not the last'.

But sometimes, even for us, it can get difficult.

Maybe we're disinclined to approach God because we feel the issue is too trivial:does God really care that my goldfish is unwell? Or maybe we fret that we don't know the right way to ask, can't find the fine words that will get us God's attention and consideration.

But the point of friendship is that we don't have to stand on ceremony; don't have to find exactly the right words; don't have to worry that it will all be too trivial.

Even if our friend thinks any or all these things, they'll help simply because we've asked. Because our friends love and care about us.

And God loves and cares about us.

It's not the *manner* of asking him that's important, it's the act of asking.

Lord, hear my prayer

What is this story saying to me, here and now?

A DRAMATIC NIGHT AT THE OSCARS

We all know people who are overly full of themselves. Jesus told this story especially for them:

At the very front table in the room the famous young actor smiled. Held court. Savoured the atmosphere. Sipped the fine champagne. Smiled at the cameras. Relished the attention. Graciously acknowledged those around him.

How he loved being centre stage. How he loved his admirers. And they him. This was going to be his moment and his alone.

'The Oscar for Best Actor goes to...'

He rose. He froze.

At the very back of the room sat an ageing Slav actor.

He froze. He rose.

The spotlights swivelled. The cameras hunted.

The old man walked the length of the room.

As he reached the front he glanced left.

Two pairs of eyes engaged.

Humility met humiliation.

Humiliation blinked.

The parable of the places of honour at the wedding feast

Luke 14:7–11

[7] *When he noticed how the guests picked the places of honour at the table, he told them this parable:* [8] *'When someone invites you to a wedding feast, do not take the place of honour, for a person more distinguished than you may have been invited.* [9] *If so, the host who invited both of you will come and say to you, "Give this person your seat." Then, humiliated, you will have to take the least important place.* [10] *But when you are invited, take the lowest place, so that when your host comes, he will say to you, "Friend, move up to a better place." Then you will be honoured in the presence of all the other guests.* [11] *For all those who exalt themselves will be humbled, and those who humble themselves will be exalted.'*

> *For all those who exalt themselves will be humbled, and those who humble themselves will be exalted*
>
> LUKE 14:11

So, what's this story saying to us, here and now?

You are who you are.

This little story is of massive relevance to us today.

It flies like an arrow to the heart of our culture.

A culture which lauds 'success' and condemns 'failure'.

A culture which assumes the logical career progression to be incessantly upwards.

What you are is more important than who you are.

But no company or team or army is 100% composed of high flyers.

And high flyers have to accept that one day someone will fly higher than them.

Who you are is as important as what you are.

Our media are tuned into and turned on by success.

We live in the age of 'celebrity'.

But the media love to debunk a celebrity who has become overly full of themselves.

How they are is more important than what they are.

Once in a while, someone emerges whose celebrity stems from their humility and integrity.

Gandhi, Mandela, the Queen, Pope Francis, Obama, Jonny Wilkinson, Steven Gerrard.

How they are is as important as who they are.

But such people also exist in every city, town, village and local community.

They are hard to find because they don't 'big-up' what they do.

They work quietly, behind the scenes. In hospitals, care homes, hospices, local charities and social centres.

In years gone by, they'd have also gone to war, prepared to sacrifice their lives in service to their country.

How they are defines who and what they are.

Volunteers.

These are the unpaid and often unsung heroes of our age.

If you are lucky enough to know one, why not try and find a way to show them your appreciation?

REFLECTION AND PRAYER

Who do I really
admire, and why?

What is this story saying to me, here and now?

THE FREE LUNCH

A lot of eating and drinking goes on in the Bible. Here's a story about a feast that Jesus told whilst at the dinner table:

The human volcano that was Aldo Cabrera threatened imminent eruption.

'How dare they insult me like this. It is a personal insult. I cannot, will not, accept it.'

The waiters, wisely, kept a discreet distance from the pyroclastic cloud.

Aldo was one of Mexico's pre-eminent chefs with a string of restaurants, signature dishes and cookbooks to his name.

Excited by the number of Brits that queued nightly to get into his restaurants in Cancun, Playa del Carmen and Puerto Vallarta, he was about to open a restaurant in London.

Acting on a suggestion from his marketing manager he had invited food critics and journalists to a private preview lunch the day before the official opening.

And that day had now arrived.

But Aldo had just been informed that most of those invited had not bothered to reply to the invitation, and all those that had done so had declined, citing a variety of prior engagements and family commitments. The pick of the bunch was a journalist who had just taken delivery of his new Porsche and, forgoing the lunch, was driving it to Silverstone for a track day.

Like many creatively endowed people Aldo's talent was accompanied by a tempestuous personality – and in his case one with a distinctly Latin flavour.

So, the answer 'nobody' to his query as to how many were likely to come, caused Mount Aldo to finally blow its top.

'It's an insult,' he roared' 'A personal insult. In Mexico they would be clamouring for a place at one of my tables, yet here I have nearly 50 covers that will go to waste.'

Then, miraculously, the lava flow stopped as a smile spread slowly over his face. 'I have an idea. My food may not be good enough for the pampered paparazzi, but it will certainly be appreciated by those who have nothing.'

He singled out three waiters:'You, you and you go and round up the homeless people in the local area.' 'Yes, boss,' they said 'but we're unlikely to find 50 of them at this time of day.' Aldo summoned two other waiters. 'In which case you and you, go to the hospital and invite patients, medicos, visitors. Lay on taxis if need be.

'I want my restaurant to be packed this lunchtime with people who appreciate and enjoy it.'

'And Alan,' he said, grabbing his hapless marketing manager by the lapels, 'you make sure that none of those ungrateful press reptiles gets to come into any of my restaurants. Anywhere, ever.'

The parable of the great banquet

Luke 14:15–24

¹⁵ *When one of those at the table with him heard this, he said to Jesus, 'Blessed is the one who will eat at the feast in the kingdom of God.'*

¹⁶ *Jesus replied:'A certain man was preparing a great banquet and invited many guests. ¹⁷ At the time of the banquet he sent his servant to tell those who had been invited, "Come, for everything is now ready."*

¹⁸ *'But they all alike began to make excuses. The first said, "I have just bought a field, and I must go and see it. Please excuse me."*

¹⁹ *'Another said, "I have just bought five yoke of oxen, and I'm on my way to try them out. Please excuse me."*

²⁰ *'Still another said, "I just got married, so I can't come."*

²¹ *'The servant came back and reported this to his master. Then the owner of the house became angry and ordered his servant, "Go out quickly into the streets and alleys of the town and bring in the poor, the crippled, the blind and the lame."*

²² *"'Sir," the servant said, "what you ordered has been done, but there is still room."*

²³ *'Then the master told his servant, "Go out to the roads and country lanes and compel them to come in, so that my house will be full. ²⁴ I tell you, not one of those who were invited will get a taste of my banquet."'*

> *Blessed is the one who will eat at the feast in the kingdom of God*
> LUKE 14:15

So, what's this story saying to us, here and now?

When I was an ad agency CEO, my diary was full.

Lots of meetings. Sometimes meetings about meetings.

On one ridiculous occasion, I realised I was in a meeting about a meeting about a meeting.

But the gaps between the meetings were also full:mainly meetings with food. I would have a breakfast, lunch or dinner scheduled each day; on many days breakfast and lunch; and quite frequently breakfast, lunch and dinner.

More meals than you could shake a stick at. With clients, colleagues, suppliers, journalists, prospective employees, heads of rival agencies. Such a busy diary meant that these were booked weeks in advance.

Sometimes a lunch had to be re-arranged because another appointment came up with a greater priority. In such cases, it was best to be honest and tell the other party the truth. It was accepted procedure, just a consequence of doing business.

But sometimes I would look at the next day's appointments and my heart would sink. What seemed like a sensible appointment to schedule six weeks earlier, now looked to be just a complete pain in the bottom. Maybe it was unfortunate timing. Or maybe I was just feeling dog-tired and unsociable. Either way, I had other things I would rather be doing. So, my PA would be given the task of calling and postponing the appointment to get me off the hook. I would tell myself that it was just business and a postponement, not a cancellation. But, I would still feel a pang of guilt.

So, this parable resonates with me, but not necessarily in a good way.

In another parable Jesus told about a great banquet, the invited guests simply did not arrive.

Here, they at least make excuses. Some may have been genuine. Some were certainly invented. The journalists' PAs were earning their wages that day.

But in the story, the invitation to the meal is an analogy for Jesus' invitation to us to follow him. Which ranks it far above a simple business or even social meeting. This is an invitation to a life-changing, life-securing meeting. There is nothing more important; nothing that should cause us to decline, postpone or cancel the invite.

If you've been prevaricating, or know someone else who has, make sure that invitation to meet with Jesus is accepted pronto.

When can I squeeze
Jesus in?

What is this story saying to me, here and now?

THE TALE OF THE NO-GOOD DO-GOODERS

When we commit ourselves to Jesus, we need to understand what a commitment it is, as these two uncompromising stories make clear:

The door opened, and the wind howled by. From this height, the curvature of the earth was clearly discernible. Gaps in the clouds afforded glimpses of the ground 5,000 feet, nearly one mile, below.

Terrified, Mo froze. This hadn't been in the script.

Certainly not when he had woken up one sunny morning, after a good night on the town, and thought to himself:'I want to do a skydive.'

A lot of his mates had done one, and dined out on the experience afterwards, so it couldn't be that difficult.

And it wasn't. One phone call to the local hospice had them biting his hand off. They would organise everything. All he needed to do was gather sponsors and turn up on the day.

Getting sponsored was not a problem. Mo had lots of well-connected and well-heeled friends. And he came from a large family, none of whom was short of a bob or two. So, the money poured in. When he told the hospice that pledges had topped £25,000 they were ecstatic.

And it didn't stop there. Hannah, his PA, organised a 'see Mo di(v)e' barbecue and disco at the airfield. With tickets priced at £100 a pop, sales quickly topped £7,500 with more expected on the day.

For once in his life, Mo felt really good about himself.

But now, as he recoiled from the plane's door and the gaping void below, all he felt was fear.

It was a tandem dive, so his dive-partner was behind him. His voice came over the intercom:'Come on Mo, just step out of the plane.'

But Mo pushed himself back. This one small step was a giant leap too far, something he had not expected.

And something he knew he could not commit himself to.

'I can't do that. Please just push me.'

'Sorry,' said the instructor, 'we're not allowed to do that. It has to be your decision.'

'Well I'm also sorry,' said Mo 'but there's no way I'm going to step out of this plane until it is sitting on the ground.'

And so, the plane returned. With Mo still firmly ensconced within it.

His friends were not impressed. His PA quit. His family were embarrassed. And the hospice had to kiss goodbye to a £35,000 donation.

Apart from her embarrassment over Mo's non-jump, Hannah, by now his ex-PA had a different problem.

Inspired by Mo, she had, on the spur of a moment, decided to pursue a girlhood dream to be part of a four-woman bobsleigh team doing the famed Cresta run.

It turned out that three of her friends were winter sports fanatics and shared the same dream.

As two of them were teachers they all decided it would be best to do it during the February half-term holiday week.

So, Hannah had snapped into action, obtained details of flights and hotel, and enrolled them at a nearby gym that was linked with a ski slope and specialised in training people for winter sports.

They commenced a gruelling 12-week fitness programme and attended weekly lectures from an Olympic bobsleigh medal winner.

At the end of the programme the four girls came together over a meal to review plans.

Hannah opened proceedings. 'So, guys, where are we at?'

'Well, we've booked our flights and hotel for that half-term week,' her three friends replied. 'What day are we doing the run?'

'Gosh, you certainly are keen beanies aren't you,' laughed Hannah.

'No, just sensible,' came the reply. 'It's half-term week, so flight and hotel availability will be limited and really expensive if you leave it too late. Have you not booked yet?'

'Um, no actually,' came the reply.

'Well that's just stupid. It cost us £1,500 each booking in advance – you'll probably have to pay double that now. And what date have you booked the run for?'

'Errrr,' said Hannah. 'Do you need to book it? I thought you just turned up and waited your go.'

'Of course you need to book it, you muppet. It's in high demand and it's not cheap at the best of times. Probably about £1,000 each for a three-run routine.'

'Whaaat!' shrieked a horrified Hannah. 'That means I'll have to spend at least £4,000, maybe closer to £5,000. That's my life savings.'

'Well, it's also your life-dream isn't it? It's ours as well, which is why we have already stumped up.'

'Noooo,' Hannah shrieked again. 'No way am I going to do that. I need that money for my wedding and house deposit. I'm sorry, but you three will have to do it without me.'

'Hannah,' they replied, 'the three of us can't do that.'

'Why not?'

'The clue's in the name, you airhead. It's a four-woman bob.'

'Well, find someone else,' countered Hannah.

'That's impossible at this stage. You have to do it with us.'

'Well, I can't and I won't. I'm as disappointed as you. I'm sorry because I know I'm letting you down, but I'm mostly letting myself down, which in many ways is worse.'

'No, it's not, you deluded featherbrain, you are mostly letting *us* down. It's not going to cost *you* a penny. We're the ones who are going to be considerably out of pocket once we've paid the cancellation fees on flights and hotels.

'Not to mention the loss of our dream.

'All because you won't honour your commitment.'

The parable of counting the cost

Luke 14:25–33

25 Large crowds were travelling with Jesus, and turning to them he said: 26 'If anyone comes to me and does not hate father and mother, wife and children, brothers and sisters – yes, even their own life – such a person cannot be my disciple. 27 And whoever does not carry their cross and follow me cannot be my disciple.

28 'Suppose one of you wants to build a tower. Won't you first sit down and estimate the cost to see if you have enough money to complete it? 29 For if you lay the foundation and are not able to finish it, everyone who sees it will ridicule you, 30 saying, "This person began to build and wasn't able to finish."

31 'Or suppose a king is about to go to war against another king. Won't he first sit down and consider whether he is able with ten thousand men to oppose the one coming against him with twenty thousand? 32 If he is not able, he will send a delegation while the other is still a long way off and will ask for terms of peace. 33 In the same way, those of you who do not give up everything you have cannot be my disciples.'

And whoever does not carry their cross and follow me cannot be my disciple

LUKE 14:27

So, what's this story saying to us, here and now?

The invitation to follow Christ is freely and unconditionally given.

'Come as you are' is the invitation.

Acceptance is also easy. There is no complicated and long-winded application system. No interview to prep for. No references to provide.

The decision to follow Christ is a life-saving, life-gaining one.

But.

It's also a life-changing one.

Not one to be taken on a whim, or fad or flight of fancy,

It's a real commitment.

It challenges and changes lifestyle priorities

On the surface, it may seem a small step, but it is actually a huge leap with big consequences: *"those of you who do not give up everything they have cannot be my disciples"*.

Having invited Jesus into our life, we then need to be prepared to turn that life over to him.

As Captain James T Kirk would (ungrammatically) put it: 'to boldly go'.

Even to the point of making a one-mile jump or blowing our life's savings.

But the prize is huge: the achievement of our real life-dream.

Our eternal life-dream.

REFLECTION AND PRAYER

Am I boldly going?

What is this story saying to me, here and now?

LOST (AND FOUND)

In Luke's Gospel (Chapter 15) Jesus recounts three consecutive stories about three things being lost:a sheep, a coin, a son.

Each lost item is dearly loved, and sadly missed, by the person who lost it.

In each case the lost item is subsequently found and returned to its rightful place; and the owner's sense of loss is replaced by great joy.

It was clearly a message that Jesus wanted to be sure to get across.

THE TALE OF THE MISSING PUPIL

Jesus had been talking about the need for people to re-think faith issues. To forgo the prevailing legalistic mindset, and approach it anew through the eyes of a child. To illustrate this, he told the famous parable of the shepherd and the lost sheep:

Ollie was tumbling in a white gyroscope.

Ollie the 'Beast of Year 9'.

Ollie was petrified.

Charlotte began the headcount.

Things had started so well.

The dawn of the ski trip in the Austrian Alps had slowly drawn its curtains on a cloudless, deep blue sky and a sparkling white snowscape.

She and the other four teachers had shepherded the kids onto the ski-bus to the base of the mountain and then onto the 2,000-feet gondola ride to the ski slopes.

Where, after the dreaded ski-off assessment run, their 100 pupil charges had been split into five groups ranked by experience and ability, each group with a local ski instructor.

Ollie couldn't stop himself falling.

Ollie the 'King of Detention'.

Ollie gasped.

The first three groups were first-timers and they were taken to the nursery slopes.

The fourth group had a couple of weeks' experience and headed off to the blue runs.

The remaining handful ventured further afield across the mountain to some stiff reds and blacks.

Charlotte, the trip leader and most experienced skier, patrolled the nursery slopes and the blue runs checking on the progress of her less experienced pupils.

Fun in the sun.

She promised herself that she would have even more fun showing her elite group the way down the black runs later in the week.

Then the weather turned.

Ollie saw his ski detach and disappear into the white.

Ollie the 'Enforcer'.

Ollie screamed.

The cloud base dropped like a doomed elevator. The bright blue sky became steely grey. A biting wind set in.

The fun disappeared.

Fortunately, the local ski instructors knew their mountain and had anticipated events. They knew it was time to get off the mountain.

Charlotte supervised the groups as they assembled at the top of the gondola.

As the three nursery groups started their descent back down, the fourth group were returning from their blue runs.

So far, so good. Ninety pupils on their way. The 10 black-runners were higher up the mountain but should be back shortly.

Ollie felt his face numbing.

Ollie the 'Teacher Tamer'.

Ollie wept.

Charlotte counted in the elite group.

...7, 8, 9.

'Where's the tenth?' she yelled at the instructor.

He looked at her blankly.

'For goodness sake,' she said and headed for the nearest ski lift.

She reached the top. It was even worse than she had feared. A complete white-out, with visibility down to a couple of yards.

There were two slopes back down the mountain Red 4 and Black

13. Reasoning that the instructor would have chosen the easier route she headed off down Red 4.

Charlotte prayed.

Ollie felt so alone.

Ollie the infamous 'One and Only'.

Ollie prayed.

Charlotte saw a dark shape just ahead and to her left.

Instinctively she stabbed her right leg, her downward ski, into the slope to come to a juddering stop, downslope of Ollie.

She reached out and grabbed him.

'Take off your ski.'

He looked at her.

'For once in your life just do as you are told.'

Ollie did as he was told.

Charlotte grabbed him. 'Stand on my skis in front of me.'

That night 99 pupils were sipping hot chocolate and swapping stories of their great adventure.

But Charlotte was still hugging her 100th charge.

Who, for the first time in his life was enjoying being teacher's pet.

The parable of the lost sheep

Luke 15:4–7

⁴'Suppose one of you has a hundred sheep and loses one of them. Doesn't he leave the ninety-nine in the open country and go after the lost sheep until he finds it? ⁵And when he finds it, he joyfully puts it on his shoulders ⁶and goes home. Then he calls his friends and neighbours together and says, "Rejoice with me; I have found my lost sheep." ⁷I tell you that in the same way there will be more rejoicing in heaven over one sinner who repents than over ninety-nine righteous persons who do not need to repent.'

The parable of the wandering sheep

Matthew 18:12–14

¹²'What do you think? If a man owns a hundred sheep, and one of them wanders away, will he not leave the ninety-nine on the hills and go to look for the one that wandered off? ¹³And if he finds it, truly I tell you, he is happier about that one sheep than about the ninety-nine that did not wander off. ¹⁴In the same way your Father in heaven is not willing that any of these little ones should perish.'

"

Rejoice with me; I have found my lost sheep

LUKE 15:6

So, what's this story saying to us, here and now?

I don't know about you, but I don't know many shepherds.

But I do know lots of teachers.

My youngest daughter, Charlotte, is one. A PE teacher. And she leads ski trips.

Which was the inspiration for my rewiring of the parable.

I don't know a lot of lost sheep either.

But I do know a lot of lost people.

We all do. The world is full of lost souls.

You and I are unlikely to be able to reach them all.

(Although, with God on our side, we should be careful never to rule anything completely out.)

But this parable talks about a particular kind of 'lost sheep'. In fact, Matthew calls it a 'wandering sheep'.

Someone who was once part of the flock, secure in the fold but is now absent.

Twenty years ago, a piece of research was done which showed that 20% of people were regular or occasional churchgoers; but that a further 20% were lapsed churchgoers who were open to the idea of returning. They had not been particularly disenchanted with their churchgoing experience, nor had they rejected their faith. For whatever reason, they had just dropped out of the habit of going.

This was an observed church-wide phenomenon.

How about your church? Has anyone stopped coming?

Maybe it has been a gradual process and they have simply dropped off the radar.

Maybe they were a bit of an Ollie.

Maybe this happened years ago.

Maybe, it's only now as you read this that you realise that you haven't seen them for a while.

Maybe you could seek them out on social media.

Or, better still, drop round and see them.

Which lost sheep
do I know?

What is this story saying to me, here and now?

THE VERY SAD (AND YET STILL HOPEFUL) STORY OF THE LOST WEDDING RING

As you'll gather from the first few words, this is clearly me speaking, not Jesus. But I think it still gets the message across:

My wife, Valerie, is extraordinarily beautiful. And kind. And forgiving (which is helpful being married to me). And organised. (Helpful again!) And loving, considerate, saintly even.

I need to get all that out of the way, because whilst it's true, it's maybe not the whole story.

She does have a short suit.

She is not the tidiest person in God's creation.

Full of the Spirit, yes. Full of the tidy-bug, no.

And the absence of the gift of tidiness (with which I am not altogether blessed either, it must be said) has led to a tendency for her to mislay things (but there we are perfectly complemented as I have the gift for finding).

So that's all good then.

With one notable and tragic exception.

Nearly 20 years after we were married she mislaid her wedding ring at our home in Kent. It was not any old ring. I had not bought it from a jewellery shop.

(Yes, her engagement ring had come from Ratners at a cost of just £13.50 – all the money I had aged 19 and yet to start a job. But that is by the by).

This wedding ring was special because it had been handed down to her from her grandmother and so was irreplaceable.

As I say, I have been blessed with the gift of finding so I knew all would be well.

But, more than 20 years later, I'm still searching.

Gold is virtually indestructible. And it doesn't tarnish or deteriorate. So, the galling thing is that we both know it exists somewhere, shiny, waiting to be discovered.

It may be that thousands of years from now it is retrieved from the ditch or jackdaw nest in which it has laid secreted for millennia and a bald-domed Time Team are interpreting it.

She has a new ring now, blessed and dedicated at our silver wedding anniversary. But equally we both still live in hope that, one day, we may find the original.

And, if we do, I can promise you that we shall have the party to end all parties!

The parable of the lost coin

Luke 15:8-10

[8] *'Or suppose a woman has ten silver coins and loses one. Doesn't she light a lamp, sweep the house and search carefully until she finds it?* [9] *And when she finds it, she calls her friends and neighbours together and says, "Rejoice with me; I have found my lost coin."* [10] *In the same way, I tell you, there is rejoicing in the presence of the angels of God over one sinner who repents.'*

> *And when she finds it, she calls her friends and neighbours together and says, "Rejoice with me; I have found my lost coin"*
>
> LUKE 15:9

So, what's this story saying to us, here and now?

What I really like about the 'lost parables' is that the protagonist does not sit still, passively bemoaning their loss. They search desperately for it.

Here, the woman turns her house upside down to find her lost coin.

Elsewhere, the shepherd heads for the hills to hunt for his lost sheep.

The father looks out every day for his errant son, and when he sees him in the distance rushes out to meet him and bring him home.

And, 20 years on, Valerie and I are still hunting for her ring.

How wonderful to think that God is desperately looking for each and every one of his prodigal children.

If, in this strange world of spiritual sardines that so many of us choose to play you've not let him find you yet, maybe it's time to come out from behind the couch. Be assured, he's not going to give up looking.

In fact, he'll do whatever it takes. 2,000 years ago, he even took on human form.

And maybe he's asking you or me to help him find someone in particular today.

How hard am I
searching?

What is this story saying to me, here and now?

THE TALE OF THE TEENAGE WASTREL

This third parable in the 'Lost' sequence is about a lost son; lost to his father and lost to himself:

If you ever find yourself in the backstreets of Oldham, try to find your way to Clarendon Street and have a look at a garage you'll find there: Butterworth and Co. Apart from being an honest, well-run, family business, it has an interesting story to tell.

The father, John, worked hard throughout the eighties and nineties to build his business, which acquired a strong reputation for restoring and maintaining classic cars. Ferraris, Porsches and, their speciality, American Mustangs and Cobras. Granted, there weren't too many of these sorts of cars cruising around the streets of Oldham, but they required specialist mechanics and there weren't too many of those around either! His two offspring, Sharon and Lee learned these specialist skills alongside their father and the plan was to expand the business, with Sharon and Lee each opening their own outlets, funded by their father.

John found their first suitable site, in Leeds, and Sharon set to work. It was hard going but she stuck at it. Signs were that in a few years it would be a very profitable business. Meanwhile John had identified another site, this one in Liverpool and earmarked it for Lee when his apprenticeship was finished.

But Lee had other ideas. Fired by the Mustangs and Cobras his mind was set on Los Angeles. A cool city with lots of classic cars on the streets. On his 18th birthday, and without saying anything to his father or Sharon, he transferred £200,000 from the company's business bank account into his personal account. 'I'm of age now, and it will be mine anyway when the old man dies,' he reasoned, 'so it's only like he's died a bit before his time.'

So, Lee set off for the big time. And he loved it. He found premises in Beverly Hills, much more expensive than he had anticipated, but what the heck, looking at the number of classic cars adorning the streets, the money would soon be rolling in. And what a place to live! Girls, restaurants, a classic car of his own, and Las Vegas just a four-hour drive across the desert. He'd never experienced the delights of blackjack, fine champagne and a blonde on his arm in Oldham! He hired some experienced mechanics to do the grubby work, whilst he concentrated on flying the high life.

But a time bomb was ticking. Whereas he had been well apprenticed in the art of servicing classic cars, no-one had taken Lee though the intricacies of the cash flows, profit and loss summaries and balance sheets involved in running a business. And whilst he had slavered over the sight of so many classic cars on the street, he had not realised that the consequence would be a plethora of garages specialising in restoring and maintaining them.

Whilst he was running up a personal debt mountain in Vegas as a consequence of a cocktail of hotel bills, gambling losses and the expenses of a growing drink and drugs addiction; his business ran into the red, ran out of cash and ran up losses that its assets would not cover. In short, he was bankrupt. Worse than that, he was in hock to Caesar's Palace to the tune of thousands of dollars. He thought of contacting his father, but shame and fear of what he would say prevented him. He would just have to take what was coming to him.

In LA his business was liquidated by the authorities. In Vegas his passport was confiscated, and he agreed to do a five-year custodial stint in the kitchens of Caesar's Palace to pay off a small proportion of his debts there. Every day he cursed the boyish naivety that had led him into this mess and every day he wondered how his father and elder sister were getting on back home. At this point, even Oldham sounded attractive.

He wrote regularly and whilst he gave no hint of the actual state of affairs, especially his current incarceration, he resolved that once he had completed his five years, he would return home. After all, he reasoned, the only job he knew was restoring classic cars and as his future now lay in working for someone else, he may as well do that to help his father's business.

Come the day, he bought a cut-price single airfare to Manchester and wrote to his father to let him know he would be coming back and explaining all the circumstances.

Arriving at Ringway Airport he was surprised and amazed to see his father waiting for him at the Arrivals barrier, carrying a big 'welcome home' sign. Which he dropped as soon as he saw his son, vaulting the barriers and running down the Arrivals hall, dodging other arriving passengers as he did so.

In a scene that could have been cut directly from 'Love Actually' father and son fell into each other's arms. 'Dad, I feel so stupid and so ashamed. I've wasted all the money you worked so hard to make. I know it's all my own fault and I wouldn't blame you at all if you just told me to get lost, but can I just come back and work for you? I probably won't ever be able to pay it all back, but at least I can give it a go.'

To Lee's utter amazement, all his father did was to hug him tighter and cry a little. Wiping away the tears he replied 'Yes, of course you can come back. Forget about the money, it's not important. We'll create another pot of capital for you and before too long you'll be up and running in Liverpool or wherever else you like. Meanwhile, I have that bottle of vintage champagne your grandfather left me on ice at home, so let's get back and get stuck in.'

Back home, Lee found a big welcome party waiting to greet him. He disappeared upstairs to drop his things in his old room. Meanwhile, Sharon accosted her father. 'Dad, what on earth are you on? Lee robs you of your cash, deserts us to run off to the States, and has a fine old time whilst I've been working round the clock to help you build the business. Not once have we stopped to celebrate like this. What's got into you?'

'Sharon,' his father replied, 'I know what you're saying and why. I really do love and appreciate you. This business is as much yours as mine. But I thought I'd lost my son, your brother, and I'm just so glad he's back. I can't think of much else I'd rather celebrate more.'

The parable of the prodigal son

Luke 15:11–32

[11] Jesus continued,'There was a man who had two sons. [12] The younger one said to his father, "Father, give me my share of the estate." So he divided his property between them.

[13] 'Not long after that, the younger son got together all he had, set off for a distant country and there squandered his wealth in wild living. [14] After he had spent everything, there was a severe famine in that whole country, and he began to be in need. [15] So he went and hired himself out to a citizen of that country, who sent him to his fields to feed pigs. [16] He longed to fill his stomach with the pods that the pigs were eating, but no one gave him anything.

[17] 'When he came to his senses, he said, "How many of my father's hired servants have food to spare, and here I am starving to death! [18] I will set out and go back to my father and say to him:Father, I have sinned against heaven and against you. [19] I am no longer worthy to be called your son; make me like one of your hired servants." [20] So he got up and went to his father.

'But while he was still a long way off, his father saw him and was filled with compassion for him; he ran to his son, threw his arms round him and kissed him.

[21] 'The son said to him, "Father, I have sinned against heaven and against you. I am no longer worthy to be called your son."

[22] 'But the father said to his servants, "Quick! Bring the best robe and put it on him. Put a ring on his finger and sandals on his feet. [23] Bring the fattened calf and kill it. Let's have a feast and celebrate. [24] For this son of mine was dead and is alive again; he was lost and is found." So they began to celebrate.

[25] 'Meanwhile, the elder son was in the field. When he came near the house, he heard music and dancing. [26] So he called one of the servants and asked him what was going on. [27] "Your brother has come," he replied, "and your father has killed the fattened calf because he has him back safe and sound."

[28] 'The elder brother became angry and refused to go in. So his father went out and pleaded with him. [29] But he answered his father, "Look! All these years I've been slaving for you and never disobeyed your orders. Yet you never gave me even a young goat so I could celebrate with my friends. [30] But when this son of yours who has squandered your property with prostitutes comes home, you kill the fattened calf for him!"

[31] "'My son," the father said, "you are always with me, and everything I have is yours. [32] But we had to celebrate and be glad, because this brother of yours was dead and is alive again; he was lost and is found."'

So, what's this story saying to us, here and now?

This is one of the best-known parables.

Some people find it helpful to look at it from the absconding son's perspective; others from the father's; and others from the elder son's (or, in the case of my rewiring, the elder sister's.) Some people like to take their time and consider it from all three points of view.

See which works best for you.

For me, there is one strong and central message that stands out.

However far you may feel that you have drifted away from God, there is always a way back. And moreover, he is constantly looking out for you and will even come to meet you.

Like many people I first encountered God as a child. I had a Bible and went to Sunday school. But, when I started to become more independent as an older teenager, I began to drift away. God no longer seemed so relevant to my life. And when I packed my bags and left home to start work, I also packed my spiritual bags and put them in storage.

But, twenty years later, a set of circumstances caused me to dig out those bags and head back to God. And there he was, waiting for me, as if I'd never been away. Actually, he wasn't just waiting, I sensed him running towards me with as many tears in his eyes as I had in mine.

All I had to do was say 'I'm sorry' and God took it from there.

There must be millions of people in our country that have not rejected God, but simply drifted away from him.

If you are one of them, then this parable is for you.

There must be millions more who feel they have offended God or are just not good enough to be accepted by him.

If you are one of them, this parable is for you also.

God wants you back home with him.

All it takes is a meaningful 'sorry' (or as the Bible puts it elsewhere 'a broken heart and a contrite spirit').

How far from home
am I?

(I'm sorry, Lord)

What is this story saying to me, here and now?

(LOST) AND FOUND

To be completely and utterly lost can be profoundly disturbing.

Equally, to lose something precious can be profoundly distressing.

These parables enable us to experience the sense of loss from both perspectives.

I remember once losing touch with my young daughter, Georgina, in a crowd.

She freaked out and I freaked out.

When reunited we were both in tears.

When we lose touch with God it disturbs us.

When we lose touch with God it distresses him.

The good thing is that God never loses touch with us.

So, there is always a way back.

And he is always there, waiting.

THE STORY OF THE SASSY THEME PARK MANAGER

Jesus told some really extraordinary stories. Take this one for instance:

'The King of Fun.' That's what they call Albert Tomkins.

Born in the first half of the 20th century, he has managed to stretch himself out towards his centenary in the 21st.

He claims he has now forgotten more than he ever learned, but the lie of that can be found in the way that, even in his 92nd year, he keeps a tight grip upon his business empire.

Maybe that is because his empire is all about fun. Fun parks to be exact.

Of which he has six, dotted around the country.

But not all at the moment are fun. In fact, one is being a real pain.

The park in Margate is seeing admissions down, revenues down and profit wiped out.

Sure, there are mitigating circumstances:weather, poor transport links, competition, the economy. But Albert never has been or ever will be the mitigating type.

So, Miranda Sherburn, the commercial manager of the park, knew she was on an increasingly sticky wicket.

Albert had made this clear:'Write your profit up or your resignation down, lass. You have four weeks.'

Miranda was in despair. The operational product:rides, catering and so forth, was controlled centrally, she had no input to that. And so too were the admission prices. She could not affect those.

Or could she??

She was desperate. She could feel the axe blade, cold upon her neck. OK, she thought, I can't change prices, but I could change our rebate policy. I'm not really sure I'm allowed to do that; in fact I'm really sure that I'm not, but what the heck. I just need to get people in here. There's no way I'll get a job elsewhere with this place looking like a locked-down city after the curfew.

So, everyone who came in was given an immediate 50% reduction on their admission fee because some parts of the park 'were still under construction'. And children under 11 were admitted free of charge.

Well, Miranda thought, it's Albert's park so it's his money. He's not going to miss a few bob. And the main thing is, if admissions pick up it will play really well on my CV when Albert sacks me for what I've done.

And, sure enough, visitors told family and friends about this fantastic value for money. A local celebrity with a large following on social media tweeted about it and liked the park's Facebook page.

Word got around, admissions increased, and Miranda didn't know whether to be pleased or terrified.

And then Albert paid a surprise visit. To inspect the books.

But to Miranda's complete surprise, he was delighted.

'Footfall,' he exclaimed. 'Admissions. Users. Whatever you want to call them. They are all on the up! Well done, my girl.

'The key to any business is to get people aware of, and interested in, your product. To persuade them to try it. Then it's down to product quality. Make that good enough, and they'll come back again. And profit will follow.

'You've created interest in this fun park. Now all we need to do is convert them into loyal, repeat customers.

'You can leave that bit to me; your job is to keep on attracting them.'

The parable of the shrewd steward

Luke 16:1-8

Jesus told his disciples: 'There was a rich man whose manager was accused of wasting his possessions. [2] *So he called him in and asked him, "What is this I hear about you? Give an account of your management, because you cannot be manager any longer."*

[3] *'The manager said to himself, "What shall I do now? My master is taking away my job. I'm not strong enough to dig, and I'm ashamed to beg –* [4] *I know what I'll do so that, when I lose my job here, people will welcome me into their houses."*

[5] *'So he called in each one of his master's debtors. He asked the first, "How much do you owe my master?"*

[6] *'"Three thousand litres of olive oil," he replied.*

'The manager told him, "Take your bill, sit down quickly, and make it fifteen hundred."

[7] *'Then he asked the second, "And how much do you owe?"*

'"Thirty tons of wheat," he replied.

'He told him, "Take your bill and make it twenty-four."

[8] *'The master commended the dishonest manager because he had acted shrewdly. For the people of this world are more shrewd in dealing with their own kind than are the people of the light.'*

> *For the people of this world are more shrewd in dealing with their own kind than are the people of the light*
>
> LUKE 16:8

So, what's this story saying to us, here and now?

What a strange parable. What an odd message.

On the surface.

The principal character is called a shrewd manager. You and I might well call her something else.

So, what point is Jesus trying to make?

Well, in my rewiring I've tried to bring out the importance of adapting central policy in the light of on-the-ground knowledge.

The big multinational marketing companies have a phrase for it:'Think global; act local'.

The church is a wonderful institution, full of devoted ministers.

But like a lot of institutions it can occasionally lose touch with life outside it.

The devoted ministers are not necessarily exposed to real world conditions on a daily basis.

Maybe you and I are better placed to speak into the workplaces and social circles that we inhabit and know first-hand.

Maybe God is calling us to say and do whatever it takes to bring people to him.

To be shrewd managers and fill his fun park.

Is my mouth
spreading the Word?
(Lord, open my lips)

What is this story saying to me, here and now?

A TALE OF TWO LANDLORDS

Many of the stories Jesus told were rooted in the ordinary; but some grew out of the extraordinary. This, in the original, is one of those and, consequently, I found it the most difficult parable to 'rewire'. I pray that I have done it justice:

In the closing years of the last century some people started to build up property portfolios. Soaring property prices meant it was a win-win game:capital appreciation and rental income.

This is a tale of two men who jumped on the bandwagon.

But with very different business philosophies.

Scrooge's objective was to make as much money as possible. Full stop. The houses and his tenants were simply a means to that end and were treated accordingly. Houses were renovated as cheaply as possible and maintained in the same way, if at all. Tenancy agreements were written entirely in Scrooge's favour allowing him to terminate and evict at will. Deposits were, of course, never returned.

Cratchit saw his purpose as providing a service to his tenants. Tenancy agreements were fair and exceeded all the legal requirements in terms of protecting tenants' rights. Houses were renovated and maintained to the highest standards. Cratchit's philosophy was to provide accommodation that he himself would be happy to live in.

Both men focussed their businesses on Canterbury, a heritage city with a large and transient student and young professional population. So, they were constantly competing for properties and tenants. Scrooge's lower renovation and non-existent maintenance costs meant that he could take great delight in gazumping Cratchit on house purchases and undercutting him on rentals. His objective was to squeeze Cratchit out of business so that he could buy up his assets at a knock-down price.

This fierce competition led both men to re-invest all their profits in their businesses.

And why not? What could possibly go wrong?

In 2007 they found out the answer to that question.

The bank-led financial crisis led to a crash in property prices and a freeze on mortgage lending.

Almost overnight win-win became lose-lose.

Many property speculators saw their businesses destroyed as banks foreclosed and crystallised negative equity. Scrooge and Cratchit were among their number. Their world moved from the benefits of business to the business of benefits.

But, just a couple of months later, Scrooge saw that Cratchit was back in the property market. He raged and cursed. How could this be?

His investigations revealed that Cratchit had received a large grant from the Property Landlords Association.

Immediately Scrooge applied and immediately he was refused. And immediately he demanded a meeting with them.

He stormed into their offices and his temper worsened as, whilst sitting in reception, he could see Cratchit through the glass walls enjoying tea and cake and talking with the Chairman in what was obviously a very affable meeting.

Scrooge was then shown into the office of the Grants Director. No tea was offered and certainly no cake. The essence of the case Scrooge made was that his business was much bigger than Cratchit's and so he should get a correspondingly larger grant.

The Grants Director was not impressed.

'The size of a business has no bearing on whether or not we make a grant. That decision is based solely on how a landlord scores in the tenant satisfaction surveys that we carry out.

'It may interest you to know that Mr Cratchit has topped that survey for the past five years and that is why we immediately gave him a grant. Half a million pounds at no interest and payable back over 20 years.' Scrooge's eyes bulged. 'Mr Cratchit is good for the reputation of our industry and we want him back in business. It may also interest you to know, Mr Scrooge, that you have been consistently bottom of our survey, by some distance. In fact, you were hardly on the scale. You, Mr Scrooge, are the type of person we do not want in our industry. You bring us all into disrepute.'

This stinging rebuke was made even more unpalatable for Scrooge by his being able to see Cratchit across the corridor taking another piece of cake and enjoying a joke with the Chairman.

He changed tack. 'Well if not me, could you make a grant to my close associates, the Marleys. My son works with them. I now understand how you see things and I shall join them to make sure they change their working practices. Please also send Cratchit to talk to them and explain how you want them to operate.'

'No, Mr Scrooge. We have talked regularly with the Marleys over the years, asking them to change their business practices. As they chose not to listen then, I see no reason why they would genuinely listen now, even if we were to send Mr Cratchit as living, breathing evidence of the value in doing so.

'Sorry Sir, there is to be no grant from this Association for you, the Marleys, or any others of your ilk.'

The parable of the rich man and Lazarus

Luke 16:19–31

19 'There was a rich man who was dressed in purple and fine linen and lived in luxury every day. 20 At his gate was laid a beggar named Lazarus, covered with sores 21 and longing to eat what fell from the rich man's table. Even the dogs came and licked his sores.

22 'The time came when the beggar died and the angels carried him to Abraham's side. The rich man also died and was buried. 23 In Hades, where he was in torment, he looked up and saw Abraham far away, with Lazarus by his side. 24 So he called to him, "Father Abraham, have pity on me and send Lazarus to dip the tip of his finger in water and cool my tongue, because I am in agony in this fire."

25 'But Abraham replied, "Son, remember that in your lifetime you received your good things, while Lazarus received bad things, but now he is comforted here and you are in agony. 26 And besides all this, between us and you a great chasm has been set in place, so that those who want to go from here to you cannot, nor can anyone cross over from there to us."

27 'He answered, "Then I beg you, father, send Lazarus to my family, 28 for I have five brothers. Let him warn them, so that they will not also come to this place of torment."

29 'Abraham replied, "They have Moses and the Prophets; let them listen to them."

30 '"No, father Abraham," he said, "but if someone from the dead goes to them, they will repent."

31 'He said to him, "If they do not listen to Moses and the Prophets, they will not be convinced even if someone rises from the dead."'

> *If they do not listen to Moses and the Prophets, they will not be convinced even if someone rises from the dead*
>
> LUKE 16:31

So, what's this story saying to us, here and now?

This story has a touch of 'Tales of the Supernatural' about it.

It is also one of the harshest stories that Jesus told.

Normally he would tell people that there was still time to heed his message.

Even for the criminal who was dying on the cross next to him.

But here he is very clear that time runs out when you die. And that, once dead, you can't turn the clock back.

Most people in our country have not rejected Jesus; they have just not got around to accepting him yet.

But, the message here is stark and clear.

If you keep putting your faith decision off until tomorrow, just bear in mind that one day tomorrow won't come.

REFLECTION AND PRAYER

Is time slipping through my hands?

(carpe diem)

What is this story saying to me, here and now?

THE LABOURERS ON THE BUILDING SITE

Jesus has just been quite tough on a young man who has his priorities in life wrong, but now he can sense that his disciples are having a crisis of confidence about whether even they are good enough for Heaven. So, he tells them this story...

Tomasz Glik, the owner of a building construction firm in Portsmouth, was delighted to win the contract for a new sports and leisure centre. The first task was to prepare the site. Not as easy as it might sound since it was previously occupied by a pig farm, and dozens of concrete sties still littered the area in varying states of disrepair. Moreover, access was restricted, making it impossible to get the normal earth-moving machinery onto the site. This was a job for good old-fashioned grunt work! And so, Tomasz put the word about that he was on the lookout for a few heavies. He was keen to get the site cleared and he reckoned a day's blitz on the site should do it.

Early the next morning he found a dozen men outside the site. They agreed a rate of £80 for the day's work and they got themselves stuck in. By the time the first tea break came around it was clear that these guys were good workers. It was equally clear, however, that there weren't enough of them to finish the job that day. So, Tomasz took a stroll into town and found the local jobcentre. There were another dozen men there that fitted the bill so he signed them on, agreeing that, although they would not be doing a full day, he would nevertheless pay them a fair rate.

It then rained, turning the site into glue and making it obvious that yet more manpower would be required. Tomasz went back into town and found half a dozen Polish workers in a cafe. Two further trips to a couple of pubs generated another ten, a mix of Bulgarians, Romanians and Latvians. But late in the day he knew he needed a final boost for the last couple of hours. He found his labour in the shape of five strapping young local lads returning from a day's fishing. It did the trick. By the time the light was failing at 9.00pm the site was clear.

Tomasz called his foreman over and asked him to pay the labourers starting with the last ones 'recruited' and going onto the first.

The foreman gave £80 to each of the young lads who had been nobbled on their return from their fishing trip. At this, the early morning starters became very excited as they anticipated a bumper payout. But when the foreman came to them he gave each of them £80 also. They sought out Tomasz to register their dissatisfaction. 'What's the game? The guys you brought on site at the end of the day only worked a couple of hours, but you've treated them the same as us and we worked through the whole day, rain and all. That can't be fair.'

'Hold on' said Tomasz, 'I'm not being unfair to you. I agreed to pay you £80 and that's what I've done. You were OK with that then and you should be OK with it now. If I want to be generous and give the lads who came last the same amount, surely that's my concern. It's my money and I'm just pleased we all got the job done together.'

The parable of the workers in the vineyard

Matthew 20:1–16

'For the kingdom of heaven is like a landowner who went out early in the morning to hire workers for his vineyard. ² He agreed to pay them a denarius for the day and sent them into his vineyard.

³ 'About nine in the morning he went out and saw others standing in the marketplace doing nothing. ⁴ He told them, "You also go and work in my vineyard, and I will pay you whatever is right." ⁵ So they went.

'He went out again about noon and about three in the afternoon and did the same thing. ⁶ About five in the afternoon he went out and found still others standing around. He asked them, "Why have you been standing here all day long doing nothing?"

⁷ '"Because no one has hired us," they answered.

'He said to them, "You also go and work in my vineyard."

⁸ 'When evening came, the owner of the vineyard said to his foreman, "Call the workers and pay them their wages, beginning with the last ones hired and going on to the first."

⁹ 'The workers who were hired about five in the afternoon came and each received a denarius. ¹⁰ So when those came who were hired first, they expected to receive more. But each one of them also received a denarius. ¹¹ When they received it, they began to grumble against the landowner. ¹² "These who were hired last worked only one hour," they said, "and you have made them equal to us who have borne the burden of the work and the heat of the day."

¹³ 'But he answered one of them, "I am not being unfair to you, friend. Didn't you agree to work for a denarius? ¹⁴ Take your pay and go. I want to give the one who was hired last the same as I gave you. ¹⁵ Don't I have the right to do what I want with my own money? Or are you envious because I am generous?"

16 'So the last will be first, and the first will be last.'

> So the last will be first, and the first will be last
> **MATTHEW 20:16**

So, what's this story saying to us, here and now?

Lots of things.

First thought. In God's eyes, people are valued in the absolute terms of their own worth rather than relative to others.

The last can indeed be first and the first last – except that with God there is no first and last!

Those of us who are Christians should try and value people likewise. It is not for us to judge or condemn, to say who is or isn't worthy of Heaven. It is for us to encourage and welcome.

And if ever we measure ourselves against others we invariably invite trouble:berating ourselves for not being as good as them; or condemning them as not being as good as us.

God values everyone equally, so maybe we should do the same.

Second thought. Heaven has no maximum capacity and 'latecomers' are welcomed every bit as much as the 'earlybirds'.

In the story, the latecomers onto the vineyard and building site could easily have said 'no' because they were too tired, had better things to do, wanted to eat, or simply because they'd had a rubbish day and it sounded too much like hard work. And they may have thought there would not be enough money in it to make it worthwhile anyway. But they chose to say 'yes' and gained a reward as good as the early arrivals.

No-one is ever too late or too old to become a Christian.

As the thief crucified alongside Jesus discovered.

Third thought. Heaven is not an 'exclusive' establishment.

We cannot earn or buy our way in. 'Entry' is completely at God's discretion, by his grace.

Unlike the local golf or yacht club, there is no selection committee; no people we need to curry favour with; no waiting lists; no priority applications. It's open to all who have put their faith and trust in Jesus.

Fourth thought. There is no 'queue' for Heaven.

Because God searches us out, knocks on the door of our heart and invites us in.

In fact, he never stops knocking.

If you haven't yet heard him, listen up!

REFLECTION AND PRAYER

Is Heaven knock,
knock, knocking at
my door?

What is this story saying to me, here and now?

THE REFEREE'S TALE

Jesus spent three years with his twelve disciples, a really extended coaching session! He knew that the future of the church depended on these guys. Here's something he taught them about prayer:

Mike Blackwell shivered, checked his watch, tested his whistle and looked around.

A hundred spectators? Maybe 150.

A far cry from the 75,000 or more, just two weeks ago.

But that had been in Auckland. Where he had refereed the Rugby World Cup semi-final:South Africa taking on France.

Whereas Vigo Village versus New Ash Green in the Kent 3rd League was never going to attract the world's media. Particularly on a mudbath of a pitch under unremittingly grey and freezing skies.

But this was where he had refereed his first game 20 years ago to the day, and so he had accepted an invitation to return and referee this local village derby to mark the occasion.

It was good to return to his roots and he was looking forward to a couple of convivial pints with some old friends in the club bar afterwards.

An hour later, a mediocre game was nearing the final quarter and Mike was anticipating his hot shower when one of the New Ash Green wingers intercepted a pass and sprinted for the Vigo line. With only the full back to beat, he body-swerved but then crashed to the ground.

Mike's whistle shrieked long and hard. He sprinted across to the Vigo number 15, scowling and flourishing his red card. A trip was unacceptable at any level of the game. Not in Auckland. Not at Twickenham. Not at Murrayfield. And not here.

The player protested that he had not touched the winger; that his opponent had beaten him all ends up but then slipped in the mud at the end of the body swerve.

Mike would have none of it.

The player's team-mates furiously claimed there had been no physical contact.

Mike would have none of it:he was used to team pressure.

A group of spectators joined the protest.

Again, Mike would have none of it:they were clearly biased to the home player.

The New Ash Green winger took Mike to one side and explained that he felt he had simply slipped.

Still, Mike would have none of it:he knew what he had seen. It was a trip.

And he was an international panel referee. One of the top refs in the world. There was no way he could get such a decision wrong.

Except that, in this case, he had.

The Vigo full back was waiting outside the clubhouse after the game and again pleaded his innocence.

Mike's response was to inform him he would be reporting him to the Rugby Union and that he could expect a lengthy ban.

When Mike emerged from his dressing room it was to find the distraught full back with several of his teammates in support.

Mike resolutely turned his back on them and headed for the bar.

He was halfway through his first pint when the Vigo deputation again appeared, this time swelled by several spectators all claiming that Mike had made a grave error.

Mike started to lose his temper and when a group of New Ash Green players joined the dissent against his decision he exploded and stormed out towards his car.

But once outside he reflected. Top international ref he might be, but the level of protest was passionate, widespread and seemingly sincere. Plus, not one voice had been raised in support of his decision. Maybe, just maybe, he had got this one wrong.

Time for some grace and humility.

Mike returned to the clubhouse bar. 'Normally, TV cameras would be used to review my decision but clearly we don't have that luxury here. However, I guess human eyes can be as good as any technology and I have been swayed by your consistency, unanimity and sheer persistence. I therefore reverse my decision. The next round is on me.'

The parable of the persistent widow

Luke 18:1–7

Then Jesus told his disciples a parable to show them that they should always pray and not give up. ² He said:'In a certain town there was a judge who neither feared God nor cared what people thought. ³ And there was a widow in that town who kept coming to him with the plea, "Grant me justice against my adversary."

⁴ 'For some time he refused. But finally he said to himself, "Even though I don't fear God or care what people think, ⁵ yet because this widow keeps bothering me, I will see that she gets justice, so that she won't eventually come and attack me!"'

⁶ And the Lord said, 'Listen to what the unjust judge says. ⁷ And will not God bring about justice for his chosen ones, who cry out to him day and night? Will he keep putting them off? ⁸ I tell you, he will see that they get justice, and quickly. However, when the Son of Man comes, will he find faith on the earth?'

> *And will not God bring about justice for his chosen ones, who cry out to him day and night? Will he keep putting them off?*
> LUKE 18:7

So, what's this story saying to us, here and now?

It's always great to talk about answered prayer isn't it? So we tend to make a point of sharing our answered prayers with others.

But we are never quite so keen to talk about our unanswered prayers.

Some people will say that there is no such thing as unanswered prayer.

But in this parable, Jesus is urging his disciples to be persistent in their prayers. To pray, pray and pray again. If they need to keep on praying it means that the prayer has not yet been answered.

Why might that be?

I can suggest several reasons.

Maybe it's because the answer doesn't come in the timescale we expect. So, when we do get to see it, we don't realise that it is an answer to that particular prayer.

Maybe the answer doesn't come in the manner we expect. So, again, we don't connect the answer with the prayer request.

Maybe God wants us to continue praying because that is helpful for us. Prayer is a conversation with God, so prolonged prayer may not be such a bad thing! People of strong faith are invariably people of strong prayer and vice versa.

Maybe something is getting in the way.

Parents will know the problems of dealing with a disobedient or rebellious child. 'Sorry before please' is often the response to a plea for a new toy or late night pass.

Is there anything we need to say sorry to God about before we say please?

Maybe it's because of a lack of real faith on our part.

Are we praying more in hope than expectation? Do we definitely expect to get an answer?

Very often we can only see our prayers answered in hindsight. In different ways or timescales. And answered in the context of God's agenda, not our own.

All of which is a good incentive to be persistent in prayer.

I can look back on lots of rapidly answered prayers. And that gives me confidence in prayer. It gives me the motivation to pray.

But there have also been plenty of times when I have not witnessed an answer to my prayers, at least in the timescale or in the way that I envisaged.

I then have to work very hard not to blame myself, or God, for that. I have to tell myself to have faith that the prayer has been or will be answered, but maybe in a way I cannot see or comprehend.

However, I have also realised that there is another reason why I may not get the answer to my prayer.

Maybe I am being too self-centred. Not selfish, but self-centred. Jesus said:'I will give you anything you ask for in my name.' Have I considered my prayer from God's perspective?

Maybe, just maybe, I have asked for something that isn't good for me or runs counter to God's plans. And who am I to question the validity of those plans?

Jesus was very clear about the power of prayer.

But he was also very clear that prayer is not a slot machine. Request in; answer out. It requires real effort and perseverance on our part.

In the garden of Gethsemane, Jesus himself prayed the same prayer three times. Luke tells us that he prayed so earnestly that 'his sweat was like drops of blood falling to the ground'.

Hence this parable.

I can tell you though, that I am absolutely certain that there is no such thing as an unheard prayer.

And that is as good a reason as any to be persistent.

Should parents do everything their kids ask them to do?

(Should we expect God to do everything we ask him to do?)

What is this story saying to me, here and now?

JOUSTING ON THE HUSTINGS

'A very good evening to you and thanks for tuning into Metro Radio here in the North East.

It's our 60-second sound-off.

A minute-long popularity-pleading slug-fest.

The by-election happens in just a couple of weeks, so tonight we hear from our two leading candidates.

First up will be Rhys Evans, a prominent local businessman – many of us will have bought or sold properties through his estate agency.

And following him Rav Kapoor, manager of a local bank – your overdrafts are in his hands.

Remember the golden rule guys:60 seconds max, so make it count.

Rhys, let's have you first.'

"My record speaks for itself. I'm honest, trustworthy, fair-dealing. My word is my bond. Not at all like the other sharks in my trade. And certainly not like this greedy banker. Check me out on Google:I give loads to charity. Vote for me and you'll have a proven winner as your MP."

'OK Rhys, thanks. Rav, your turn.'

"I've always tried to use the money entrusted to me wisely and responsibly. I know I haven't always got it right, and I'm really sorry about that. But I'll keep striving for economic and social fairness if you'll let me."

'Thanks guys. Let's take a look at the online feedback.

Well, it looks like Rav is the clear winner tonight. Roll on the election.

Next up we have the new Sunderland manager telling us why they won't be involved in the relegation battle this season....'

The parable of the Pharisee and the tax collector

Luke 18:9–14

⁹ *To some who were confident of their own righteousness and looked down on everyone else, Jesus told this parable:*

¹⁰ *'Two men went up to the temple to pray, one a Pharisee and the other a tax collector.* ¹¹ *The Pharisee stood by himself and prayed:"God, I thank you that I am not like other people – robbers, evildoers, adulterers – or even like this tax collector.* ¹² *I fast twice a week and give a tenth of all I get."*

¹³ *'But the tax collector stood at a distance. He would not even look up to heaven, but beat his breast and said, "God, have mercy on me, a sinner."*

¹⁴ *'I tell you that this man, rather than the other, went home justified before God. For all those who exalt themselves will be humbled, and those who humble themselves will be exalted.'*

For all those who exalt themselves will be humbled, and those who humble themselves will be exalted
LUKE 18:14

So, what's this story saying to us, here and now?

It cuts straight to the heart of the nature of our attitudes to, and relationships with, other people.

We live in an era of self-sufficiency. From an early age, we are taught the importance of standing on our own two feet. To be confident and assertive. Our abilities are regularly tested at school and the results held up for all to see. Under-performance is not permissible:poor exam results reflect upon both pupil and teacher.

Successful sportspeople, entrepreneurs and entertainers are held up as role models.

Self-belief is seen as the key to such success.

The problem comes when self-belief turns to belief in self. When we start believing our own publicity. When we become seduced by our own infallibility. When we become arrogant towards, and dismissive of, those around us.

In the original parable, it is likely that neither the Pharisee nor the tax collector were particularly popular people. The former was typically religiously arrogant; and the latter would probably have cheated his neighbours.

In similar fashion, neither estate agents nor bankers top the public popularity charts (a reflection on the perceptions of the professions, rather than the people involved I hasten to add!).

And here we have representatives of each profession seeking to become politicians, another profession that struggles to win public affection.

But we see a marked difference in the attitudes between Rhys and Rav. One projects self and puts others down; the other espouses service and mutuality. I know who would get my vote.

Elsewhere in the Bible, Jesus was very clear that, before we criticise others, we need to take a long hard look at ourselves. Planks in the eye and all that.

In many ways, we are defined by the nature of our relationships with other people.

It is this that creates our true legacy.

Is there a plank in
my eye?

What is this story saying to me, here and now?

THE STORE MANAGERS

Gregor Macpherson was a shrewd and successful retailer.

Hard dealing, but fair, he had started his first computer supplies shop in Glasgow in 1998, capitalising upon the rapidly growing interest in the internet and computing in general.

An outstandingly successful first couple of years was followed by two of famine as the dotcom boom turned so spectacularly to bust. For a while, Gregor's business looked set to follow so many others into receivership. But Gregor was a fighter. Street-fighting retail tactics helped him weather the storm.

By 2004 the business was back on track and Gregor had opened another two stores. His experiences of the early years had not left him, however, and he was known for his cautious and hard-nosed approach to business, judiciously balancing risk and reward.

Then a year later disaster struck again. But of a very different form than five years earlier. Gregor was diagnosed with cancer. There was a ray of light. The doctors were optimistic about Gregor's chances. However, he would require surgery followed by an extended period of complete rest.

Gregor's fighting spirit roared into action. He summoned his three store managers and gave each autonomous control over their stores. Then, after a successful surgical procedure, he followed the doctors' advice and moved to Fiji for a year's rest. The managers were instructed to run their stores as if they were their own businesses and under no circumstances to contact Gregor.

Two of the managers embraced the opportunity enthusiastically. This was their chance to shine.

Pritti launched a laptop repair service which was an immediate success. Ewan trimmed his range, cut his costs and lowered his prices. This also reaped immediate rewards.

In contrast, the third manager, Duncan, was worried. 'Gregor will be furious if anything goes wrong,' he said to himself. 'Best to play things safe.' And so he changed nothing. And so nothing changed.

After his year's sabbatical, Gregor returned. Full of vim and vigour. And a sense of his own mortality which had spurred a desire to do more of what he was good at whilst he was still able to do so. In short, to open more shops.

He called his three managers together.

'Okey-dokey, let's see where we're at.'

Immediately, Pritti pushed forward. 'The laptop repair service was a real winner, boss. The business has rocketed. It's five times bigger.'

'That's fantastic, Pritti,' Gregor replied. 'I always wanted to do that but didn't have the techie know-how. I'm giving you a 25% stake in the business and I want you to implement the repair service across all shops.'

Ewan then chipped in. 'I don't have Prit's technical expertise, she's way ahead of me on that, but I do know the benefit of focusing on the best-selling lines. Profits have doubled.'

'You're so right, Ewan. Focus is everything,' said Gregor. 'You'll have a 10% stake and become our Operations Manager across the whole business.'

The spotlight fell upon Duncan. 'Mr Johnson, I know you are a hard-nosed businessman who will not accept failure. So I thought it would be best to play it safe. The store is just as you left it.'

Gregor snapped back:'Being hard-nosed doesn't make me hard-hearted. But in your case I'm going to make an exception. You should at least have raised prices in line with inflation. And you should have bought in a stock of the newer technology – your store completely missed out on the tablet market.'

'Pritti, take Duncan's store and convert it into a central base for the laptop repair service.

'Duncan, there's no place in this business for those not looking to face the risks involved in growth. I want your desk cleared and you gone within the hour.'

The parable of the talents

Matthew 25:14–30

14 'Again, it will be like a man going on a journey, who called his servants and entrusted his wealth to them. 15 To one he gave five bags of gold, to another two bags, and to another one bag, each according to his ability. Then he went on his journey. 16 The man who had received five bags of gold went at once and put his money to work and gained five bags more. 17 So also, the one with two bags of gold gained two more. 18 But the man who had received one bag went off, dug a hole in the ground and hid his master's money.

19 'After a long time the master of those servants returned and settled accounts with them. 20 The man who had received five bags of gold brought the other five. "Master," he said, "you entrusted me with five bags of gold. See, I have gained five more."

21 'His master replied, "Well done, good and faithful servant! You have been faithful with a few things; I will put you in charge of many things. Come and share your master's happiness!"

22 'The man with two bags of gold also came. "Master," he said, "you entrusted me with two bags of gold; see, I have gained two more."

23 'His master replied, "Well done, good and faithful servant! You have been faithful with a few things; I will put you in charge of many things. Come and share your master's happiness!"

24 'Then the man who had received one bag of gold came. "Master," he said, "I knew that you are a hard man, harvesting where you have not sown and gathering where you have not scattered seed. 25 So I was afraid and went out and hid your gold in the ground. See, here is what belongs to you."

26 'His master replied, "You wicked, lazy servant! So you knew that I harvest where I have not sown and gather where I have not scattered seed? 27 Well then, you should have put my money on deposit with the bankers, so that when I returned I would have received it back with interest.

28 '"So take the bag of gold from him and give it to the one who has ten bags. 29 For whoever has will be given more, and they will have an abundance. Whoever does not have, even what they have will be taken from them. 30 And throw that worthless servant outside, into the darkness, where there will be weeping and gnashing of teeth."'

The parable of the ten minas

Luke 19:11–27

[11] While they were listening to this, he went on to tell them a parable, because he was near Jerusalem and the people thought that the kingdom of God was going to appear at once. [12] He said:'A man of noble birth went to a distant country to have himself appointed king and then to return. [13] So he called ten of his servants and gave them ten minas. "Put this money to work," he said, "until I come back."

[14] 'But his subjects hated him and sent a delegation after him to say, "We don't want this man to be our king."

[15] 'He was made king, however, and returned home. Then he sent for the servants to whom he had given the money, in order to find out what they had gained with it.

[16] 'The first one came and said, "Sir, your mina has earned ten more."

[17] '"Well done, my good servant!" his master replied. "Because you have been trustworthy in a very small matter, take charge of ten cities."

[18] 'The second came and said, "Sir, your mina has earned five more."

[19] 'His master answered, "You take charge of five cities."

[20] 'Then another servant came and said, "Sir, here is your mina; I have kept it laid away in a piece of cloth. [21] I was afraid of you, because you are a hard man. You take out what you did not put in and reap what you did not sow."

[22] 'His master replied, "I will judge you by your own words, you wicked servant! You knew, did you, that I am a hard man, taking out what I did not put in, and reaping what I did not sow? [23] Why then didn't you put my money on deposit, so that when I came back, I could have collected it with interest?"

[24] 'Then he said to those standing by, "Take his mina away from him and give it to the one who has ten minas."

[25] '"Sir," they said, "he already has ten!"

[26] 'He replied, "I tell you that to everyone who has, more will be given, but as for the one who has nothing, even what they have will be taken away. [27] But those enemies of mine who did not want me to be king over them – bring them here and kill them in front of me."'

So, what's this story saying to us, here and now?

At the time of the telling of this parable, Jesus was on the road towards Jerusalem. Towards his crucifixion and the end of his time with his disciples.

So, his teaching was becoming ever more urgent.

I preached on it one Pentecost, so clearly the gift we were focussing upon then was the Holy Spirit.

And, whilst preparing my talk, I became aware that the talents that Jesus was talking about in this story were the gifts that we receive from the Holy Spirit.

I also became aware that, whilst the parable urges us to use the gifts we are given, it doesn't say how. Which is why it features three men with bags of gold; three store managers with different skills and stores.

And maybe that's because there are many different gifts given by the Holy Spirit; given to many different people; given to use in many different ways.

So, it's up to each of us to find our own gift, and use it in our own way.

And it's pretty important that we do.

In my sermon, I gave my opinion that the central thrust of this parable was summed up in verse 29:'For whoever has will be given more, and they will have an abundance. Whoever does not have, even what they have will be taken from them.'

In today's parlance that would translate as:'Use it or Lose it'.

Wow! Taken in the context of the gifts of the Holy Spirit, that's pretty dramatic isn't it? There is little that is more urgent for us to comprehend.

The thing is, each one of us has been given a gift that God wants us to use to help him further his plans. From hospitality and encouragement to prophecy and preaching. From cookery and gardening to writing and arithmetic.

Sometimes the gift is obvious. Sometimes it's not obvious to us, but is to others.

So, our task is twofold. To discern what our gifting is. And then to discern how God wants us to use it.

To best illustrate that in my talk, I found myself telling my own parable...

The Bishop's tale

HEALTH WARNING:this is a story of my own invention; not one based upon any of the parables told by Jesus.

But, I think it's worth telling, nevertheless…

A Bishop was addressing a group of sixth-formers at his local school's speech day and prize-giving.

He had been asked to offer them some career advice.

So, he told this story.

'King Edward VI Grammar School in Southampton is justifiably proud of its cricketing heritage.

They are regular winners of the Hampshire county competition and eleven times national champions.

Their golden era started in 1960 when they discovered three outstanding youngsters in the Year 6 intake:Joe, a bowler; Rashid a batsman; and Clive a wicketkeeper/ batsman.

As the trio progressed through school, the trophies flowed and they were national champions for four consecutive years.

But, in 1967, the boys' time at the school came to an end. All had done well in their A-levels and now they had career choices to make.

Joe had no hesitation in committing himself to cricket. Already on the county's books he turned full-time professional. At 20 he was selected for England. By his late-thirties he had played over 100 tests, 40 of them as captain. He retired on his 40th birthday and joined the BBC's Test Match Special commentary team.

Rashid decided to go into journalism. Starting with the Southampton Echo, he was able to continue his cricket at club and county level. He was tipped to join his friend Joe in the England team, but instead he accepted the position as cricket correspondent for the Daily Telegraph. His journalistic career flourished and, aged 37, he became the youngest ever Sports Editor of the Daily Mail.

Clive was offered a place at Christ Church College, Oxford to read law. Graduating with a First he became a lawyer and, at the unprecedented age of 32, became a QC and then a High Court judge. He still found the time to play club cricket and, on being voted President of his club, sponsored the establishment of a youth academy which went on to produce two England test players.'

After he had finished telling this story the Bishop's first question was:which of the three made the most of his natural gift for cricket?

Quickly the answer came back from the students:'Joe.'

'You have answered correctly,' the Bishop responded.

His second question was:which of the three made the most of his life?

There was a hubbub of conversation and heated debate, at the end of which the Head Boy rose to his feet:'We don't know.'

'Indeed,' said the Bishop, 'that's not so easy is it?

'The answer is that they all did, but they made different life choices.

'They used their cricketing gift differently, but they did indeed each use it.'

Later that evening at dinner, the Bishop found himself sitting next to Canon Peter Thompson, the Head of Divinity at the school.

'I have a question for you, Bishop:Christians have received the gift of the Holy Spirit, how would you advise them to use that?'

The Bishop set down his glass, bowed his head and thought carefully before responding in a reflective manner.

'That my dear Peter,' he said gravely 'is an exceedingly good question, maybe indeed life's most important question.

'Yes, all Christians have the gift of the Holy Spirit, freely given, with no strings attached. But that gift must be opened and used, and it is up to each of us to decide how to do so.

'Many Christians, perhaps indeed most, just get on with their lives, simply trusting in the Spirit and knowing that salvation is secure. There is no sin in this, although they may miss out on some of the riches on offer, much like a talented soprano deciding not to join a choir. My advice to them:that's fine, but try to allow the Spirit to work freely in your life.

'Some will combine it with other life choices. A teacher may also become a lay preacher; a successful businessperson a philanthropist; a marketing consultant may help a Christian charity. To them I say:well done, but make sure to seek out and rely on the Spirit in all you do.

'And a few will dedicate their working lives to letting the Holy Spirit work in and through them, becoming ministers, missionaries or doing other types of full-time Christian work. And my word to them is:you have chosen the hard and narrow path so always seek to grow further in the Spirit.'

The Bishop paused, sipped his wine and looked directly at Peter.

'The important thing is that, as Christians, we should always acknowledge, accept and act on the Holy Spirit's presence and gifting in our lives.'

Then he added with a rueful smile,

'And it may also be that we change our life choice as time goes by. Indeed, I myself used to be an executive for a well-known international petroleum company....'

How would you feel if you bought someone an expensive gift which they never opened?

(Jesus paid with his life to give us the gift of the Holy Spirit)

What is this story saying to me, here and now?

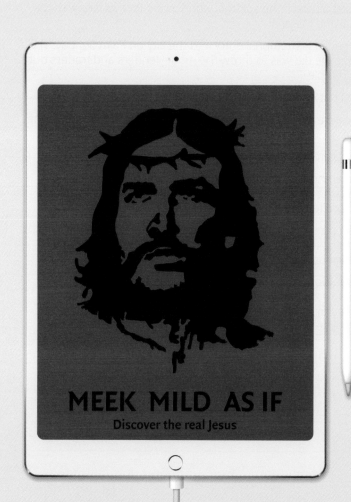

MEEK MILD AS IF

Discover the real Jesus

MEEK, MILD, AS IF...

At this point in his ministerial journey Jesus reached Jerusalem.

The point at which the spiritual world stood face to face with the physical and material.

Jesus made his triumphal entry into the city on Palm Sunday. The first thing he did was to throw the moneylenders and traders out of the Temple.

This did not endear him to the authorities.

They were even less impressed when Jesus began teaching in the Temple.

The problem was that people seemed to like him.

So, the authorities challenged him by asking him by what authority he acted. Jesus' reply was an absolute masterstroke. Make sure to read it in Matthew 21:23–27.

He then pressed home his advantage with these three parables, each one a thinly disguised attack upon the Jewish authorities and religious leaders.

Those authorities knew exactly what Jesus was doing but were unable to stop him because of his popularity with the crowds. How they must have seethed and inwardly raged. But there was nothing else they could do. For now...

STORY 1: A TALE OF TWO PLUMBERS

A TALE OF TWO PLUMBERS

Jesus started his attack with this story:

Here's something I want you to really think about.

Ramesh and Neelima were not happy bunnies.

It was the morning of February 8th.

The coldest day of the winter thus far.

And their boiler had just expired.

There was one bright spot on their horizon.

They had two sons.

And both were plumbers.

Ramesh called his elder son, Ishaan.

'I'm really sorry Dad, but I'm in the middle of a big installation and there's no way I can get around today.'

'OK, no sweat Ishaan, I'll call Dhruv.'

He had more luck this time.

'No problem. I'm just finishing up a boiler service, so I'll be with you this afternoon.'

Come five o'clock, Ramesh and Neelima were still shivering.

No sign of Dhruv.

And no answer from his mobile.

Although Ramesh did get to leave an irate voicemail.

Then, just as he hung up, Ishaan's van pulled up outside the house.

'Hey, Dad. I felt really bad at letting you down, so I've just popped round to see if Dhruv needs a hand.'

An hour later the boiler was up and running again.

So, the question is simply this: who did what his Dad wanted, Ishaan or Dhruv?

Ishaan', came the reply.

The parable of the two sons

Matthew 21:28–32

28 'What do you think? There was a man who had two sons. He went to the first and said, "Son, go and work today in the vineyard."

29 '"I will not," he answered, but later he changed his mind and went.

30 'Then the father went to the other son and said the same thing. He answered, "I will, sir," but he did not go.

31 'Which of the two did what his father wanted?'

'The first,' they answered.

Jesus said to them, 'Truly I tell you, the tax collectors and the prostitutes are entering the kingdom of God ahead of you. 32 For John came to you to show you the way of righteousness, and you did not believe him, but the tax collectors and the prostitutes did. And even after you saw this, you did not repent and believe him.'

Jesus said to them, 'Truly I tell you, the tax collectors and the prostitutes are entering the kingdom of God ahead of you
MATTHEW 21:31

So, what's this story saying to us, here and now?

These three stories are a little different in that they were aimed very specifically at a certain group of people. A group that Jesus regarded as being, at best, complacent or worse, hypocritical.

But that doesn't mean that they have nothing to say to us, here and now.

We're not told why Dhruv didn't turn up to mend the boiler, or why the son failed to go and work in the vineyard.

Nor are we told why their respective brothers changed their minds.

The reasons are not important. What is important is that actions speak louder than words.

John the Baptist was widely respected as a prophet, bearing the word of God. A strong call to everyone to repent. To own up to any spiritual shortcomings, to say sorry to God and to make a real effort to change.

Jesus' shocking message to the chief priests was that they were spiritually outranked by two of the most despised elements of society:tax collectors and prostitutes. Why? Simply because they had heard John and acted on his message; whereas the priests had heard but, for whatever reason, not acted.

The adage says that Jesus came to comfort the disturbed and to disturb the comfortable.

That is as true today as it was then. It's all too easy to become a little too comfortable in one's faith; to be long on good intentions and short on practical actions.

Do all my good
intentions result in
good actions?

What is this story saying to me, here and now?

STORY 2: THE REBELLIOUS BOARD

THE REBELLIOUS BOARD

Jesus continued his attack on the authorities by telling this very pointed story, which greatly angered them:

Yemi Jackson had founded and built up a highly successful design company that worked for many blue-chip retailers and manufacturers. It had made her a millionaire several times over. She then got a hankering to turn her talent upon the publishing business in the USA.

So, she struck an arrangement with the directors of the company, which involved selling them 25% of the business with options to buy a further 50% over time. She would remove herself from the operational side of the company and step down from the Board to become a sleeping investor. The company would belong to her former directors and employees to do with as they wished.

And so, she headed off to the Big Apple where her blend of warm humanity coated by an assertive, armour-plated business acumen made her a huge success.

But, back in the design company things were not so sweetness and light. Oh, sure it continued to be successful. Indeed, it grew. But the culture had changed. Particularly in the way it treated its staff. The directors became greedy. Bonuses were withheld, staffing levels reduced, working hours increased, salary reviews postponed. Some employees wrote to Yemi. Moved by this unrest in her 'baby' she asked the directors to amend these practices and keep faith with the staff. They responded by firing the employees who had written to her.

Shocked by this, Yemi asked some of her old, but trusted, senior managers to intercede on her behalf. Aggrieved by this apparent 'interference', the directors fired these managers also and then voted to reduce the dividend to external shareholders (ie Yemi). Feeling this to be a breach of company law, Yemi exercised the right she had retained to appoint a Non-Executive Director to the Board of the company to represent her interests. She sent her son in this capacity, feeling that he would command more respect than an unknown outsider would. Not at all deterred by this, the other directors immediately voted him off the Board.

At which point, Yemi's patience ran out. She returned to the UK, called an extraordinary shareholders meeting, re-assumed direct day-to-day control of the company, fired the entire Board and appointed a whole new set of directors to run the business.

The parable of the tenants

Matthew 21:33–46

33 'Listen to another parable:there was a landowner who planted a vineyard. He put a wall round it, dug a winepress in it and built a watchtower. Then he rented the vineyard to some farmers and moved to another place. 34 When the harvest time approached, he sent his servants to the tenants to collect his fruit.

35 'The tenants seized his servants; they beat one, killed another, and stoned a third. 36 Then he sent other servants to them, more than the first time, and the tenants treated them in the same way. 37 Last of all, he sent his son to them. "They will respect my son," he said.

38 'But when the tenants saw the son, they said to each other, "This is the heir. Come, let's kill him and take his inheritance." 39 So they took him and threw him out of the vineyard and killed him.

40 'Therefore, when the owner of the vineyard comes, what will he do to those tenants?'

41 'He will bring those wretches to a wretched end,' they replied, 'and he will rent the vineyard to other tenants, who will give him his share of the crop at harvest time.'

42 Jesus said to them, 'Have you never read in the Scriptures:

"The stone the builders rejected
has become the cornerstone;
the Lord has done this,
and it is marvellous in our eyes"?

43 'Therefore I tell you that the kingdom of God will be taken away from you and given to a people who will produce its fruit. 44 Anyone who falls on this stone will be broken to pieces; anyone on whom it falls will be crushed.'

45 When the chief priests and the Pharisees heard Jesus' parables, they knew he was talking about them. 46 They looked for a way to arrest him, but they were afraid of the crowd because the people held that he was a prophet.

Mark 12:1–12

Jesus then began to speak to them in parables:'A man planted a vineyard. He put a wall round it, dug a pit for the winepress and built a watchtower. Then he rented the vineyard to some farmers and moved to another place. ²At harvest time he sent a servant to the tenants to collect from them some of the fruit of the vineyard. ³But they seized him, beat him and sent him away empty-handed. ⁴Then he sent another servant to them; they struck this man on the head and treated him shamefully. ⁵He sent still another, and that one they killed. He sent many others; some of them they beat, others they killed.

⁶'He had one left to send, a son, whom he loved. He sent him last of all, saying, "They will respect my son."

⁷'But the tenants said to one another, "This is the heir. Come, let's kill him, and the inheritance will be ours." ⁸So they took him and killed him, and threw him out of the vineyard.

⁹'What then will the owner of the vineyard do? He will come and kill those tenants and give the vineyard to others. ¹⁰Haven't you read this passage of Scripture:

"'The stone the builders rejected
has become the cornerstone;
¹¹the Lord has done this,
and it is marvellous in our eyes"?'

¹²Then the chief priests, the teachers of the law and the elders looked for a way to arrest him because they knew he had spoken the parable against them. But they were afraid of the crowd; so they left him and went away.

Luke 20:9–19

⁹ He went on to tell the people this parable:'A man planted a vineyard, rented it to some farmers and went away for a long time. ¹⁰ At harvest time he sent a servant to the tenants so they would give him some of the fruit of the vineyard. But the tenants beat him and sent him away empty-handed. ¹¹ He sent another servant, but that one also they beat and treated shamefully and sent away empty-handed. ¹² He sent still a third, and they wounded him and threw him out.

¹³ 'Then the owner of the vineyard said, "What shall I do? I will send my son, whom I love; perhaps they will respect him."

¹⁴ 'But when the tenants saw him, they talked the matter over. "This is the heir," they said. "Let's kill him, and the inheritance will be ours." ¹⁵ So they threw him out of the vineyard and killed him.

'What then will the owner of the vineyard do to them? ¹⁶ He will come and kill those tenants and give the vineyard to others.'

When the people heard this, they said, 'God forbid!'

¹⁷ Jesus looked directly at them and asked, 'Then what is the meaning of that which is written:

"The stone the builders rejected has become the cornerstone"?

¹⁸ Everyone who falls on that stone will be broken to pieces; anyone on whom it falls will be crushed.'

¹⁹ The teachers of the law and the chief priests looked for a way to arrest him immediately, because they knew he had spoken this parable against them. But they were afraid of the people.

So, what's this story saying to us, here and now?

The ante was being upped. The authorities were now being accused not only of ignoring God's word but intimidating, punishing and even killing those who had brought it to them.

There was a historical basis for this:the Old Testament prophets had suffered greatly at the hands of the authorities. Some had been killed by them.

Jesus angered the authorities further by going on to claim that he was God's son and that they would kill him too. Which of course they did.

But what has this altercation got to do with us?

The priests were motivated by two things:a desire to protect their position and to project their worldview.

Protect and project.

We see the pattern repeated throughout our society today, in governments, political parties, commercial corporations, powerful individuals and even in church streams.

'We hold our (political/social/commercial/individual/spiritual/ theological) belief and worldview to be uniquely correct. It's the way we think, and we don't want it challenged; and we believe you should think that way too. And, if need be, we'll make you.'

Protect and project.

It seems to be endemic to the human race.

As such, each one of us individually cannot be wholly untainted. We may not have intimidated, harmed or killed in a physical sense; but there may have been times when we have done so verbally. To defend our own position or to enforce our point of view. Maybe both.

We may have done so directly, bullying. Or maybe indirectly, behind someone's back, gossiping and undermining. Which is perhaps even worse. I know that, over the years, I have been guilty on both counts.

Protect and project.

The only thing that Jesus seeks to protect is us; the only thing he projects is love.

Just saying...

Have I ever been guilty
of intimidation?

What is this story saying to me, here and now?

STORY 3: 'THE BIG MATCH'

THE BIG MATCH

The third story hammered home the last part of Jesus' attack:

In 1962 little Gordon Midgley was thrilled when his local amateur football team, Frimley Rangers, made it all the way through to the sixth round of the FA Cup. Gordon was there, draped in his red and white scarf, cheering himself hoarse and loving every second of it.

No matter that they were then blasted apart, 9–1, by the mighty Manchester United; they had tweaked the noses of the big boys and put Frimley on the map.

Little Gordon (or increasingly big Gordon as he grew in wealth, importance and weight) never forgot the thrill of that cup run and, in 2002, some forty years later, he bought the club. Over the next few years 'King Gordon', as he was known, put a lot of money into the club to bring in players and upgrade its facilities.

Imagine then Gordon's delight as, in the 2010 season, Frimley Rangers made it through to the FA Cup Third Round, the point at which the big Premier League clubs enter the competition. Would history repeat itself? Would they draw Manchester United again? Could they change history and win – or at the very least score twice – this time?

Despite all the improvements, the ground could still only hold 5,000 and there was talk of moving the venue should Frimley indeed draw one of the big clubs. But Gordon was having absolutely none of it. 'If we're drawn at home we'll be playing here. The fans will just have to diet!' Which was rich coming from 18-stone Gordon.

Tension during the draw was extreme. Frimley were seventh out of the hat – a home draw! 'YES,' yelled Gordon 'and United are still in the hat.' And United were indeed the next ball to come out, but not unfortunately the Manchester variety of United. Frimley's opposition would be Hyde United, the only other non-league team left in the cup.

Disappointment turned to despair as neighbouring Barnsley drew Manchester United at home.

But Gordon had not survived and prospered during his 45 years of life in Frimley by falling at first hurdles. 'The party's still on,' he boomed. 'We'll just have to give Hyde a good hiding – ha ha ha.'

So, the plans for the game and the associated festivities progressed and the great day dawned. With a full house of 5,000 in prospect Gordon was at the ground bright and early.

But an hour before kick-off there was hardly a soul around.

Gordon sent some ground stewards into the town to chivvy people up. But they came back puzzled. 'They don't seem to be coming.' 'Don't be stupid, of course they'll be coming,' yelled Gordon. 'Just get back there and tell them to get their backsides in gear and get along here because I've got 5,000 quality burgers for free, good beer, a rock band and the Frimley Frantic Freefall parachute team dropping by in 45 minutes.'

The hapless stewards returned to the by now deserted streets of Frimley to deliver King Gordon's invitation. 'Deserted streets' because it became apparent that a good proportion of the male population of Frimley, including just about all those who had bought tickets for the big game, had now instead decided to head off to Barnsley to see them play the other United. Two stewards tried to remonstrate with one group of fans who were on their way to the bus station, but were beaten up for their pains.

Gordon was apoplectic. 'Right, damnation to them! Just go back into town and say to anyone you find that they'll be welcome here. Anyone. Male, female, octogenarian, teenager, suckling babe, Frimley born or on a two-week heritage tour from Colombia. Just tell them we'd appreciate their support and can promise them a good time.'

And that's what happened. The ground slowly filled up and by the time of kick-off was a sea of green and white.

Gordon himself, restored to his normal indomitable good humour, roamed the ground soaking up the atmosphere, cracking jokes and leading the communal singing. He reflected that these were truly the salt of Frimley: people that really appreciated the local community and this unexpected opportunity to pull together and support it.

But then he ran into a man not wearing an inch of green or white, burping free burgers and quite obviously one or two pints of the specially brewed local ale to the worse. 'My friend,' cooed Gordon (and those who knew Gordon also knew that when he cooed it was time to check the location of the nearest nuclear fall-out shelter), 'My friend, why are you not draped in the glorious green and white of the all-conquering Frimley Rangers, and festooned with rosettes and garlands of the same ilk?'

The man was speechless (or perhaps just incapable of speech).

'Throw him out,' exploded the mercurial Gordon, 'or better still throw him in – into the nearest cesspit.'

'But, Mr Midgley,' the stewards protested, 'you invited him here.'

'Of course I invited him – I invited them all, but that doesn't mean I necessarily choose to let him stay. Now, kick him out and he can spend the rest of his life regretting the day he missed the match of the century.'

Epilogue:

Frimley beat Hyde that afternoon.

They also got to meet Manchester United that season.

At Wembley.

In the Final.

In front of 90,000 people.

And they scored two goals.

Gordon was delirious.

Unfortunately United scored five.

The parable of the wedding banquet

Matthew 22:1-14

Jesus spoke to them again in parables, saying: [2] 'The kingdom of heaven is like a king who prepared a wedding banquet for his son. [3] He sent his servants to those who had been invited to the banquet to tell them to come, but they refused to come.

[4] Then he sent some more servants and said, "Tell those who have been invited that I have prepared my dinner: My oxen and fattened cattle have been butchered, and everything is ready. Come to the wedding banquet."

[5] 'But they paid no attention and went off – one to his field, another to his business. [6] The rest seized his servants, mistreated them and killed them. [7] The king was enraged. He sent his army and destroyed those murderers and burned their city.

[8] Then he said to his servants, "The wedding banquet is ready, but those I invited did not deserve to come. [9] So go to the street corners and invite to the banquet anyone you find." [10] So the servants went out into the streets and gathered all the people they could find, the bad as well as the good, and the wedding hall was filled with guests.

[11] 'But when the king came in to see the guests, he noticed a man there who was not wearing wedding clothes. [12] He asked, "How did you get in here without wedding clothes, friend?" The man was speechless.

[13] Then the king told the attendants, "Tie him hand and foot, and throw him outside, into the darkness, where there will be weeping and gnashing of teeth."

[14] 'For many are invited, but few are chosen.'

So, what's this story saying to us, here and now?

It's a great story, isn't it? And it has a real sting in the tail. It's also one of Jesus' more multi-dimensional parables: providing messaging at many different levels. But the authorities and chief priests were no mugs; they would have understood all the messages, and all were aimed at them.

Try your own hand at hotwiring it. Pray over it and see what emerges. Then meditate upon it.

Make sure to use the notes page to jot down your thoughts.

As for me, I'm going to follow the KISS principle: 'keep it simple, stupid'. And limit myself to four short observations.

First thought. Accept the invitation.

God has invited us, through his son, to a heavenly banquet. To a party where the whole of creation – Heaven and Earth – will be renewed. Including us, together with all the believers that have preceded and will succeed us.

There is no better gig. Let's not get seduced by other attractions that are superficially glitzy, but hollow inside. And let's certainly not throw the invite into the trash can.

Second thought. Value the invitation.

Let's make sure we appreciate the uniqueness and the value of the invitation we have been given. Yes, it is given to us for free, but it has enormous face value because it was issued at great cost – Jesus' life.

Third thought. RSVP.

We have the invitation. But we must respond to it. Say 'yes', today!

Final thought. Follow the dress code

And what is that dress code?

Jesus.

We need to be clothed in Christ.

Thank you, Lord, and, yes, I'm coming.

(I'll just go and get dressed first)

What is this story saying to me, here and now?

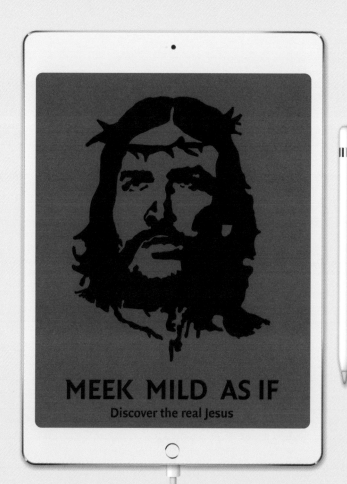

MEEK MILD AS IF
Discover the real Jesus

...MEEK, MILD, AS IF

By the time Jesus had finished telling these three stories, the authorities were livid. In desperation, they fired three, legalistically tricky, questions at him; each designed to trap him into a verbal indiscretion (Matthew 22:15–46). First the Pharisees, then the Sadducees, and then the Pharisees again. But Jesus cleverly turned the questions right back on them. And finished with a question of his own, which tied them in knots instead.

He then followed up with an astonishing verbal assault, during which he labels the authorities variously as hypocrites, blind guides, blind fools, whitewashed tombs, and a brood of vipers. He also accuses them and their predecessors of betrayal and murder. It's all recorded in Matthew Chapter 23. Do read it.

Jesus would have known exactly what he was doing: forcing the authorities into a corner. 'Back me or sack me' in our modern parlance. He would have also known the almost inevitable consequences. In the eyes and minds of the authorities, he was just too dangerous to be allowed to stick around. Like the rebellious Board and the vineyard tenants, they had too much to lose: particularly position and power.

Protect and project.

And so, the murderous plot was hatched, which would fulfil the ancient prophecies.

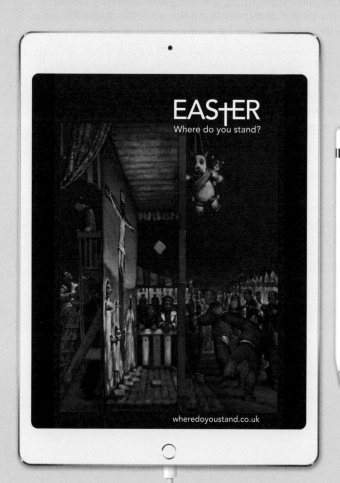

WHERE DO YOU STAND?

As he neared his crucifixion, it was only natural that Jesus would want to focus on why his physical death was necessary; what it would mean for us; the unique invitation it would create for us to follow him along the path to eternal life; and the harsh consequences for us if we fail to do so.

So, the last three parables he ever told focussed upon his return: the second coming. Each of these stories, culminating in the chilling depiction of Judgement Day, asks all people, then, now and in the times to come, one very direct question: 'Where do you stand?' It's the most important question each of us will ever have to answer...

STORY 1: TALES OF THE EXPECTED

TALES OF THE EXPECTED

Jesus' final three parables start with another typically enigmatic story. Appropriately, it's about 'the end of the age'. I've expanded it into three vignettes:

When the warm-up lap has finished and the five red lights come on over the track, you know for sure that the Grand Prix is about to start...

...once the two national anthems have been played and the All Blacks have performed the Haka, you know then that the match is about to start...

...if you hear the bell ring whilst you're in the bar at the theatre, you know that you have two minutes to get to your seat because the performance is about to start.

The parable of the fig tree

Matthew 24:32–35

[32] 'Now learn this lesson from the fig-tree:as soon as its twigs become tender and its leaves come out, you know that summer is near. [33] Even so, when you see all these things, you know that it is near, right at the door. [34] Truly I tell you, this generation will certainly not pass away until all these things have happened. [35] Heaven and earth will pass away, but my words will never pass away.'

Mark 13:28–31

[28] 'Now learn this lesson from the fig-tree:as soon as its twigs get tender and its leaves come out, you know that summer is near. [29] Even so, when you see these things happening, you know that it is near, right at the door. [30] Truly I tell you, this generation will certainly not pass away until all these things have happened. [31] Heaven and earth will pass away, but my words will never pass away.'

Luke 21:29–33

[29] He told them this parable:'Look at the fig-tree and all the trees. [30] When they sprout leaves, you can see for yourselves and know that summer is near. [31] Even so, when you see these things happening, you know that the kingdom of God is near.

[32] 'Truly I tell you, this generation will certainly not pass away until all these things have happened. [33] Heaven and earth will pass away, but my words will never pass away.'

Even so, when you see all these things, you know that it is near, right at the door
MATTHEW 24:33

So, what's this story saying to us, here and now?

Hmm, this is a tricky one. It's clearly an important parable as it's one of just seven to appear in all three of the Gospels that relate them.

Jesus told the parable in response to some specific questions from his close disciples.

He preceded it by foretelling the destruction of Jerusalem.

Not surprisingly, they were quite keen to know when that might happen.

But then they upped the ante by going on to ask what the sign would be for Jesus' second coming and the end of the age.

Well, if you were sitting in front of the man who had all the answers you'd probably ask the same things. I know I would – and a lot more besides.

The trouble is that, Jesus being the frequently enigmatic type that he was, it makes it difficult to work out which answer was being given to what question.

As a result, theologians and historians have been tying themselves in knots about it ever since.

Which, I like to think, may have been part of Jesus' intention...

But, it hasn't got me any closer to answering my own question has it? So perhaps he has snookered me as well.

For what it's worth, this is my take.

I believe Jesus would have fastened upon the really big question:how will we know when he has truly come again to make all things new?

And, in response to that, he launches into 28 verses (in Matthew's Gospel) of apocalyptic prophecy.

Read these verses. And then try and put yourselves in the position of the disciples once he had finished.

For anyone who has seen the cult film *Galaxy Quest*, there is a scene that may help.

It's the one where the crew are unexpectedly transported across the galaxy for the first time wrapped only in a kind of transparent, jelly, cling-film, bubble that on arrival upon a huge starship dissolves and leaves them as quivering, speechless wrecks.

If you've seen the film, I'm sure you will agree that helps.

If you've not seen the film, buy it!

So, confronted by his disciples' similarly shocked and stunned expressions, Jesus resorts to something more in line with their everyday experience.

The fig tree.

'Look guys, you know summer is about to start when the fig tree gets all buddy. You don't know why you know, you just know. It will be the same with my return, you'll know when you know.'

Except that, speaking personally, I wouldn't know a fig tree if it fell on me. I have oak, ash, cherry, horse chestnut and pine growing in my garden in Kent. But not a fig tree.

But I do know when the All Blacks are about to kick off; when to watch my telly so as not to miss the drama at the first corner of the Grand Prix; and when to get to my seat at the theatre. I know because I just know.

So, I'm not going to worry about exactly when Jesus is going to return.

I'll know when I know.

And I'll try to live every day as if it was going to be today.

Which is what I think Jesus may have really been getting at here, together with the implied question:'Where do *you* stand?'

What if it were today?

What is this story saying to me, here and now?

STORY 2: THE IMPATIENT PAPARAZZI

THE IMPATIENT PAPARAZZI

The can of worms had been opened. 'The end of the age' was on the conversational table. Understandably, the disciples were keen to know more about how they might prepare for it, so Jesus told them this story:

Falmouth was buzzing.

Not only did the town have a brand new sports centre on the outskirts of the town, something that the locals had been screaming for; but it was to be officially opened by global athletics superstar Nat Bulios. (A great athlete, but always inclined to get a bit mixed up.)

The big moment was set for 10am on July 18th.

A typical Cornish summer day dawned. Low scudding clouds and driving rain.

The media pack gathered early that morning at the centre. The TV camera crews led the way, starting to set up at 6am. By 8am every snack bar in the area had been cleaned out of bacon sandwiches.

The press hacks could afford to be more leisurely. And to stay dry a bit longer. They arrived outside the new centre at 9am – just in case there was an early arrival. Although the experienced ones knew there was actually more likelihood of a delay, particularly as Nat was being driven straight from Heathrow that very day.

And so it proved.

10am came and went. With no word on Nat's whereabouts. The lack of information not helped by an absence of a mobile phone signal. (Remember, this is Cornwall.) By noon, the TV boys had to pack up and go. They were scheduled to cover an important address by the Prime Minister in Cardiff later that day.

Then, just before 2pm, word began to spread that Nat would not be arriving until at least 5pm.

At which point a huge crowd of cold, wet, frustrated, annoyed, but above all, hungry hacks headed back into town to search out pasties and, whilst there, find a dry place with some landlines to take refuge within and file interim reports to their main newsdesk.

But a few local press journos from the *Falmouth Packet* and the *West Briton* remained. It was July, so local knowledge had given them the foresight to bring umbrellas. They had no main newsdesk to report to: they were it. They also knew that, in Cornwall, time is a very flexible concept. And, most importantly, and in the spirit of true Cornish people everywhere, they had brought their own pasties with them.

So, they were in exactly the right place when, at 3pm, a stretch limo arrived outside the sports centre and the unmistakable form of the great Nat Bulios unfolded itself from the back seat.

He laughed and performed his famous fake collapse. 'Well this sure is an intimate affair. Already I am loving this place.' He then grabbed a few bedraggled schoolchildren and performed his even more famous and trademark bow and arrow pose with them. After signing a flurry of soggy autograph books, he went into the sports centre. But the security men stopped the local journos from following. 'Sorry guys, the ceremony is reserved for the national TV channels.'

Nat himself interceded. 'Excuse me?? I don't see any TV cameras. I'm running well late, so I have to be out of here in an hour. These guys are here, so they get the story. Let them inside.'

As the news of Nat's arrival spread around town, the reporters from the national newspapers dropped their pasties and raced back.

As they reached the doors to the centre, the security men once again blocked their path. 'Sorry, the ceremony has started and no-one else is allowed in.'

'Don't give us that, you stupid jobsworths,' the angry hacks howled at them. 'We're from the big nationals, of course we'll be allowed in.'

One of the security men stepped to one side and talked into his radio.

After a couple of minutes, he turned back with a cheerful face. The press pack took a step forward.

'Uh-uh, not so fast people. I'm afraid it's a no-go. Nat says he doesn't care who you are or where you're from. He's given the story to the people who were good enough to be here when he arrived. Now if you'd kindly step outside gents. Oh, I see it's raining again. I hope you have your brollies with you. No? What a shame.'

The parable of the ten virgins

Matthew 25:1–13

'At that time the kingdom of heaven will be like ten virgins who took their lamps and went out to meet the bridegroom. ² Five of them were foolish and five were wise. ³ The foolish ones took their lamps but did not take any oil with them. ⁴ The wise ones, however, took oil in jars along with their lamps. ⁵ The bridegroom was a long time in coming, and they all became drowsy and fell asleep.

⁶ 'At midnight the cry rang out: "Here's the bridegroom! Come out to meet him!"

⁷ 'Then all the virgins woke up and trimmed their lamps. ⁸ The foolish ones said to the wise, "Give us some of your oil; our lamps are going out."

⁹ '"No," they replied, "there may not be enough for both us and you. Instead, go to those who sell oil and buy some for yourselves."

¹⁰ 'But while they were on their way to buy the oil, the bridegroom arrived. The virgins who were ready went in with him to the wedding banquet. And the door was shut.

¹¹ 'Later the others also came. "Lord, Lord," they said, "open the door for us!"

¹² 'But he replied, "Truly I tell you, I don't know you."

¹³ 'Therefore keep watch, because you do not know the day or the hour.'

> *Therefore keep watch, because you do not know the day or the hour*
> MATTHEW 25:13

So, what's this story saying to us, here and now?

Most of us know the date of our birthday. It forms a crucial part of our personal identity in legal terms.

It's something we use as a cause of celebration once a year.

There are other dates known to us that we also celebrate.

A wedding anniversary, Christmas, New Year's Eve, Valentine's Day, Mother's Day, Easter (although that date moves around a bit).

We are able to prepare properly for these occasions because we know that they are coming.

But a date we don't know with such advance precision is our 'deathday'.

Which may be the most important date of all, because that's when we get to meet our Lord and maker.

But, because we don't know the date, or manner, or circumstances in which we shall leave this world, it's hard to prepare for it in advance. (Apart from making a will and funeral arrangements that cater for its inevitable arrival, whenever that may be.)

And of course, we won't be there to help mark the occasion (not in any active, physical sense anyway!)

But, we will be there when we meet Jesus.

And we certainly need to be prepared for that.

But as we don't know when, where or how, we need to be constantly prepared.

And the best way to do this is by staying in a close relationship with him.

That's what this parable is saying to us here and now, today; and asking the question: 'Where do *you* stand?'

REFLECTION AND PRAYER

Am I ready?

What is this story saying to me, here and now?

STORY 3: A SHANTY OF YACHTS AND MOTORBOATS

A SHANTY OF YACHTS AND MOTORBOATS

Just as Jesus' first parable mirrored his first miracle, so it is fitting that his last parable should mirror what will be his final action:judgement.

Judgement Day is not the easiest of topics; here's how Jesus might address it:

The back of the knife struck the wine glass.

Three times, quickly.

Again.

And again.

By the time the echo of the third set of strikes had rung around the room, the post-dinner conversation had halted and the 30 pairs of eyes and ears around the U-shaped banqueting table had refocussed upon the immaculately tailored 52-year-old man who had risen from his chair.

Jules Fine was the Founder and Chairman of Fine Communications:the world's third-largest advertising, PR and marketing communications group and the only group that still remained in private ownership.

Jules was a giant of the industry, a legend. Charisma flowed from him like Vesuvian lava.

'Friends, today marks 25 years since the original Fine & Partners ad agency opened its doors for business.

'The first five years were difficult to say the least. That you can blame on me for choosing to start a business a year before a global recession. But it gave us an enormous advantage. Whilst others were cutting staff, we were adding them. We became a hothouse for talent and that powered us for the next 15 years.

'And then, five years ago, the next recession struck. Deeper and more savage than anything the world had seen before. Yet we doubled in size in the first two years and now I can tell you that we have redoubled.

'And, as members of our Worldwide Board of Directors, everyone around this table has profited.'

As he paused for a sip of water there was applause around the table and, amongst the American contingent some high-fives.

'Now I have an important task to perform.'

The room instantly quietened and swelled with pregnant expectancy.

'I have been asking myself a question:how sustainable is this success? In the history of mankind, no empire, whether business, political or military has survived indefinitely. Frequently, the peak of success heralds an imminent decline and fall. Does our recent success mask an awful truth that we may have reached the end of our life cycle?'

The atmosphere in the room changed subtly. The expectancy was shaded with uncertainty. Where was this going?

'Please look at your place cards. You'll have noticed that some are in the shape of yachts and others of motorboats. Whilst this may chime with our surroundings here in Portofino, it is not just a design conceit.

'Would all the yachts please come and stand to my right. And all motorboats to my left.'

In puzzlement and with a slight feeling of trepidation people abandoned their places at the table and gathered in the two groups, 10 to Jules' right and 20 to his left.

Jules turned to his right. 'You people have served me well and will continue to do so. You will each receive a year's salary as a bonus in reward.'

He then swivelled 180 degrees. 'I'm sorry to say that you have not served me as well and that your contracts will be honoured but terminated with immediate effect.'

Jules sat down as the room exploded. A cocktail of astonishment and shock, mixed and shaken with relief and despair.

After a few minutes the back of the knife struck the wine glass again.

This time it took five repetitions of the three-strike sequence to bring order to the room.

Jules stayed seated and looked to his right and then to his left.

'I'm guessing you want to know how I reached this decision.

'Well, I'm going to tell you.

'When I founded this company, I had a Vision. I wanted my company to be the most admired ad agency in the world; the company that people wanted to work for beyond any other.

'I then decided that the best way, the only way, that vision would be achieved was if we pursued three Values in all that we did.

'You all know these values:they should be written on your hearts:

Integrity

Humility

Compassion

'One of my favourite mottos is "what gets measured gets done". So, every year, I've conducted research to check out how we perform against these values. I have been the only person to ever see the results of this research.

'For 20 years, we received near perfect scores on all three dimensions. But over the last five years there has been a steady decline.

'So, this year I did some additional research. I asked a cross-section of our staff, our clients and our suppliers to rate each of you, individually, against our values.

'My reasoning was that each time one of our staff, clients or suppliers interacted with one of my senior leaders it should be as if they were doing so with me personally.'

He stood and faced the people on his left.

'You all fell short, far too short to remain in this company. Your continued presence would undermine all I believe in and have tried so hard to have us achieve. Please leave the room now.'

There was an uncomfortable silence and then they started to drift out.

He turned to face those who remained.

'Thank you for staying true to my values and therefore to me. I know I can trust you to take the company forward over the next 25 years. We have most certainly not reached the end of our life cycle. Indeed, if we continue to stay true to our values there will be no life cycle.

'I think a glass of champagne is in order.'

The parable of the sheep and the goats

Matthew 25:31–46

[31] 'When the Son of Man comes in his glory, and all the angels with him, he will sit on his glorious throne. [32] All the nations will be gathered before him, and he will separate the people one from another as a shepherd separates the sheep from the goats. [33] He will put the sheep on his right and the goats on his left.

[34] 'Then the King will say to those on his right, "Come, you who are blessed by my Father; take your inheritance, the kingdom prepared for you since the creation of the world. [35] For I was hungry and you gave me something to eat, I was thirsty and you gave me something to drink, I was a stranger and you invited me in, [36] I needed clothes and you clothed me, I was sick and you looked after me, I was in prison and you came to visit me."

[37] 'Then the righteous will answer him, "Lord, when did we see you hungry and feed you, or thirsty and give you something to drink? [38] When did we see you a stranger and invite you in, or needing clothes and clothe you? [39] When did we see you sick or in prison and go to visit you?"

[40] 'The King will reply, "Truly I tell you, whatever you did for one of the least of these brothers and sisters of mine, you did for me."

[41] 'Then he will say to those on his left, "Depart from me, you who are cursed, into the eternal fire prepared for the devil and his angels. [42] For I was hungry and you gave me nothing to eat, I was thirsty and you gave me nothing to drink, [43] I was a stranger and you did not invite me in, I needed clothes and you did not clothe me, I was sick and in prison and you did not look after me."

[44] 'They also will answer, "Lord, when did we see you hungry or thirsty or a stranger or needing clothes or sick or in prison, and did not help you?"

[45] 'He will reply, "Truly I tell you, whatever you did not do for one of the least of these, you did not do for me."

[46] 'Then they will go away to eternal punishment, but the righteous to eternal life.'

> *Truly I tell you, whatever you did not do for one of the least of these, you did not do for me*
> **MATTHEW 25:45**

So, what's this story saying to us, here and now?

Jules Fine is based on a real person and that is his real name. He was a great mentor to me as I progressed through the advertising business.

Of Jewish extraction and an emigrant to the USA from central Europe in the post-war years, he never got to start and run his own business, so Fine Communications is an invention. But he did get to become Vice Chairman and Strategic Director of a major global ad agency

Jules was a humble and sensitive man of great wisdom and strong values and I think he'd appreciate the role and actions I've created for him here.

In this parable, we see Jesus using a teaching style that has real edge.

Once again, there is only black and white, with a dash of hyperbole for good measure. We've seen it elsewhere. In an oral teaching tradition, Jesus was really, really keen to make sure he got his point across.

This time I've chosen not to dumb that down or introduce any shades of grey.

When we sign up to something:a cause, team, belief; we then have a choice.

Do we subscribe in words alone:armchair supporters?

Or in words and actions:an active fan base?

In modern parlance:do we choose to talk the talk, or walk the walk.

Jesus is clear:our Christian faith should permeate our whole life and influence our values, our words and, crucially, our actions.

If you want to understand more about this, read the book of James. He was Jesus' brother and was just as black and white:

What good is it, my brothers and sisters, if someone claims to have faith but has no deeds? Can such faith save them? ... As the body without the spirit is dead, so faith without deeds is dead. (James 2:14 & 26)

Clearly, the way we work out our faith in our lives is for each of us to discern and decide. Not all Christians are called to the ministry or to overseas mission. Some are called to work out their faith in sport, business, entertainment, teaching, parenting, volunteering. Some even in advertising!

The question Jesus is asking each one of us here is, whatever it is we do for a living, whether we are willing to allow our life to become a witness to him:'Where do you stand?'

REFLECTION AND PRAYER

Am I talking and
walking?

What is this story saying to me, here and now?

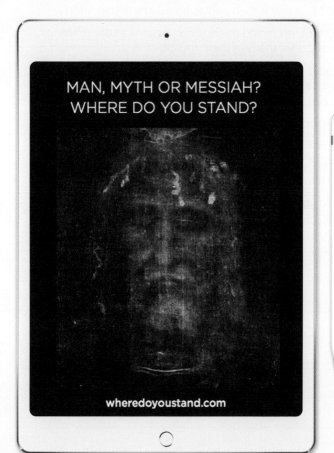

WHERE DO YOU STAND?

If you have been reading the parables sequentially, you've now reached the end.

You have travelled with Jesus through his ministry and heard his teaching as he told it then and as he may have told it today.

You may have preferred the original versions to the rewirings. That's ok: I prefer many of them myself!

But I believe it is important to keep Jesus' teaching relevant and contemporary, and I hope I have helped in that respect.

Some scholars have hailed the parables as the greatest ever teaching.

Others have dismissed them as being too contrived, or too simplistic, or irrelevant to life today.

What do you think?

Where do **you** stand?

SHARABLE PARABLES:
RIP IT UP

As you are now reading this, it may be that you've worked your way through the book. Which poses the question as to what to do with it next.

You may want to keep it on the bookshelf for future reference, for personal devotional use, or maybe even as a preaching and teaching resource.

That's fine.

Maybe you'll pass it onto a Christian friend, or donate it to your church's bookstall.

That's also fine.

Maybe you'll donate it to a local second-hand bookshop or charity shop.

That's fine too.

Maybe you'll put it in your waste bin.

That's not so fine. Please don't!

Maybe you know a non-Christian to whom one parable in particular would appeal. But you may also feel that to give them the whole book would be overkill. If that is the case, simply tear that parable out of the book and give it to them.

Sorry, Dad.

(My father was a teacher with a great love of books and, when I was a child, if I so much as creased a page I was severely chastised.)

But Dad also knew that Jesus told the parables to be heard. And to be shared.

So, rip it up. Job done.

SHARABLE PARABLES:
FILL YOUR BOOTS

Memo

To: All Preachers
From: Mike Elms
Subject: Fill Your Boots!

Content Usage Permissions

I felt that I was called by God to write this book.

It was a call that took me some years to hear; and even more to act upon.

Even then I thought: 'Why me? I have no theological qualifications, I'm not in ministry, not even an accredited author. I'm just an adman.'

And then I realised that maybe that was the point. God was choosing on the basis of practicality: what I do, rather than who I am.

For years, I have worked to bring products and services to the attention of the public: to present them in an appealing and motivating way. That has also led to me playing a part in revitalising some famous brands to keep them contemporary and front of mind: the likes of Ford, Guinness, Lucozade, Marmite. To respect their heritage and core values, but to update their communications packaging.

That was what I felt God was calling me to do with the parables in this book and I pray that I have been faithful to that calling.

Because of that, I am waiving copyright on the content. These are stories to be told and shared; not to be owned by anyone.

PTO

But with one proviso: the content cannot be used for commercial gain. The permissions of use for some of the images and storyline settings have only been granted on that basis. (Indeed, for my own part, I feel that while God is calling me to write this book, he is not calling me to profit from it. Quite the reverse in fact: I have had to make some significant investments to bring it to fruition. And in the unlikely event of there being a surplus, it will be used to help fund future projects: watch out for a contemporary look at some of the Proverbs.)

With that proviso, please feel free to use any of the stories and images in the book for preaching or otherwise sharing God's word. And if the characters, names, settings and storylines don't quite work for you, or you can see ways of 'localising' them so that they will connect more strongly with your audience, then please do so. This may particularly be the case if you do not live in the UK. I also encourage you to share your versions on the website so that others may benefit.

Good stories, like strong brands, need to evolve and adapt over time and who knows where technological and social change will take us?

Virtual reality parables maybe...

SHARABLE PARABLES:
CALLING ALL SPIDERS

I love books. They are so tactile. You can feel them, smell them, caress them, cuddle up with them, share them, read them to your kids and grandkids.

I also love my Kindle. When I travel, I can take a library with me; previously I had to take an extra suitcase. And if my mood changes or a particular book enthrals, I can instantly download an extra book or two.

At the time of writing, I'm not sure when this will be available as an e-book. It's hard to reproduce the colourful images and it's even harder for you to write on it. But I have faith in technology and the time will come.

What I do know is that its raw creative content will spin its way onto the web.

As I sign off on the printed pages I am already working on the digital ones.

All you spiders of the web can access these by using the QR code below to jump to the 'Resources' page at *www.parablesrewired.com* which is reserved for those of you who have been kind enough to buy this book.

Once there you will find downloads of the words and images, which may be helpful if you are a preacher, and a 6-part study guide for your small group, which may be similarly helpful if you are a leader.

Please do register with your email, (which will be kept strictly between you and me), because I will then be able to let you know about future developments. I'm aiming to add additional storylines; one or two videos; some feedback and share pages; plus I'm most of the way through writing my next book: 'Proverbs – Restitched in Time'.

And God has also placed in my mind: 'Pstories from Psalms'...

AFTERWORD:

Jesus told his parables to a wide range of audiences and for a variety of purposes.

He told them to his small band of disciples to encourage and train them; to vast crowds to inform and inspire them; as guidance to those genuinely seeking enlightenment; to hostile groups such as the Pharisees to chastise them; as a riposte to scheming opponents and their efforts to discredit or entrap him.

As I've been writing this book, I've found myself thinking time and again about the effect the parables would have had on these varying audiences.

Intrigued? Challenged? Shocked? Stunned? Confused? Informed? Bewildered? Enlightened? Annoyed? Enthused? Angered?

All of the above.

What they would not have been is bored or disinterested.

My aim has been to help people of today experience those parables afresh, whether hearing them for the first time or the umpteenth.

I hope that, as you've read them, you've tried to stand in the shoes of those various audiences; to project yourself into their mindsets; and that you've also tried to visualise Jesus, with all his human passion and spiritual power, standing in front of you, talking directly to you.

If not, go back and read some of them again. Not my 'rewirings', but the originals, as Jesus told them. That's why I've included them.

As with all scripture, we should expect the parables to talk to us today. I hope that, in my commentaries, I've touched on some ways in which they do this.

Clearly, I do not know all of you readers, individually and personally. So, I haven't been able to tailor my messages to each and every one of you. But Jesus does know you, intimately. And if you give him the time and space to do so, he will tell you precisely what these parables mean for you.

Finally, Jesus told his parable stories so they could be shared with and re-told to others. Particularly to those who couldn't or wouldn't come and hear them from him first-hand.

So, if you know someone who doesn't yet know Jesus, and they are someone who you feel Jesus wants to speak with, please share this book with them so he can do so!

May the grace of our Lord Jesus Christ, the love of God, and the fellowship of the Holy Spirit be with you all, now and for evermore.

Mike Elms

IF YOU HAVE ENJOYED

'PARABLES: REWIRED'

LOOK OUT FOR

Re-stitched in Time

A 21ST CENTURY JOURNEY
THROUGH PROVERBS

COMING IN 2022

FIRSTWORD

I was always of the opinion that the book of Proverbs was a collection of ancient 'stitch in time' truisms and potentially misleading 'red sky at night' snippets of country folklore.

Little there, I thought, that would be of relevance to our modern, scientifically grounded, technologically advanced society.

Even after I became a Christian it was a book in the Bible I tended to avoid.

I could see the practical application of Psalms as an aid to prayer and worship.

I could see the power of the Parables and the relevance of their messaging for us today, here and now.

But Proverbs? Past their sell-by date, surely?

Take Proverbs 28:3 for instance:

"A ruler who oppresses the poor

Is like driving rain that leaves no crops"

See what I mean. Country folklore on steroids.

Then a thought struck me.

This could have come directly from a modern business textbook.

A harsh, autocratic management regime that places the pursuit of profit beyond all else, even to the extent of exploiting its workforce and denying employee's rights is the equivalent of a ruler oppressing the poor.

And the driving rain that leaves no crops is evident in the inferior product quality, productivity and profitability that tends to emanate from such management regimes.

The business textbook would no doubt include numerous case studies to illustrate the benefits of a more enlightened management style.

But whereas the book would take two hundred pages to make the point, Proverbs 28:3 does it in two lines.

So, I thought that it was time that I took a closer look at the Book of Proverbs

And, as I read and reflected, I found that it actually focusses on eternal truths that are as applicable today to everyday relationships and practical issues as they were 3,000 years ago.

(In his Bible paraphrase, 'The Message', Eugene Petersen calls Proverbs 'A Manual for Living').

So, come with me on this journey through Proverbs and see what I mean.

SECONDWORD

FIRSTWORD

Before we set off on our journey, there's one thing I must tell you.

If you're expecting a straight line trip from Chapter 1 to 31 you're going to be disappointed.

Sure, a 3 lane motorway will generally take you to your destination faster than the B roads.

But meandering country lanes are much more interesting in terms of the scenery, sights, places and people they throw up along the way.

So, look upon this journey as more of a walking ramble.

We're going to start in Chapter 13 and then see where we go from there.

But I can tell you that, along the way, we're going to meet England footballers, world boxing champions, entrepreneurs, famous brands, African countries and spoiled children.

And much more beside.

THE JOURNEY WILL START IN 2022

'LEGAL STUFF'

First published in 2021

Christian Publishing & Outreach Ltd

1 Easting Close, Worthing, BN14 8HQ

British Library Cataloguing-in-Publication Data

A catalogue record for this book is available from the British Library

ISBN 978-1-5272-9665-7

Design and typesetting

Phill Roberts, Dan Nolloth & Tom Barnard

Cover image

Javier Martinez – Unsplash

Printing by

Christian Publishing and Outreach Ltd

www.cpo.org.uk